"In order to take steps in faithful mis
challenging context, spiritual leaders
to their own soul-care. With decades
behind them, Winfield and Mark come alongside us and gently
describe the rhythms and practices that can help us do this.
Reading their words renewed both my missional imagination
and my commitment to stay refreshed in my friendship
with Christ."

— **Trevor Hudson**, Pastor and Author, South Africa

"*Healthy Rhythms for Leaders* is a handbook for every leader
offering clear guidance for integrating spiritual practices that
are both personal and missional. I recommend that every leader
read it and share it with those they are leading!"

— **Dave Ferguson**, Lead Pastor, Community Christian
Church and Author of *B.L.E.S.S.*

"More than ever before, missional leaders need help to be able
to navigate the changes and challenges of the chaotic world we
live in. Rooted in Scripture and in the history of the church,
Bevins and Dunwoody have written a deeply spiritual and
timely resource that will help leaders thrive by promoting
healthy rhythms of spiritual and missional practices. Read it
and put it into practice!"

— **Alan Hirsch**, Author and Activist, alanhirsch.org

"I have wondered—perhaps you have too—*what happened
to people during our pandemic?* Did anxiety about the virus
overwhelm us? Did the restriction of time with others make us
happy or depress us? Or, as these wonderful authors suggest,
could we use the time to develop healthy, holy rhythms for

prayer and contemplation, and so form a rule of life? This book contains timely words for an unusual time that can become timeless."

— **Scot McKnight**, Professor of New Testament, Northern Seminary

"In this book, authors Bevins and Dunwoody serve as gentle guides, reminding us of the ancient rhythms that our overly utilitarian culture has caused us to forget. Walk with these wise authors and allow them to lead you back into a hopeful spiritual rhythm that is reliable as the tide."

— **Tracy Balzer**, Director of Christian Formation, John Brown University, and author of *A Journey of Sea and Stone: How Holy Places Guide and Renew Us*

"If you are looking for a spiritual formation resource that is personal yet communal, practical yet narrative-based, deep yet accessible . . . then you have it in this little gem. I found it helpful for me both as a pastor and as a human being."

— **A.J. Sherrill**, Author of *The Enneagram for Spiritual Formation: How Knowing Ourselves Can Make Us More Like Jesus*

"*Healthy Rhythms for Leaders* is an important book, an essential manual for anyone wanting to support leaders and multiply their effectiveness, longevity, and health. Read it, digest it, use it!"

— **Ric Thorpe**, Bishop of Islington, Gregory Center for Church Multiplication

"When I opened *Healthy Rhythms for Leaders*, I discovered a treasure chest. In its succinct pages were gems of venerable spiritual wisdom yearning to be invested in a new generation of missional pioneers. I will be telling every church planter I know about the treasure in this transformative resource."

— **Larry Walkemeyer**, Lead Pastor, Light & Life Church and Director of Equipping, Exponential

"With an understanding of the challenges in modern-day society, the authors, Winfield Bevins and Mark Dunwoody offer a fresh, inclusive approach to the contemplative journey. In the midst of a society that is inundated with doing, through them, God blesses us with life-changing rhythms of slowing."

—**Barbara L. Peacock**, Author Soul Care in African American Practice and Chair of Biblical Studies at Chun University

"I am particularly pleased to commend this strategic little book. Bevins and Dunwoody address the key issues for missional practice: The relationship between our life in God and our service of God."

— **Graham Cray**, Former Bishop of Maidstone, Archbishops' Missioner, and Leader of the Fresh Expressions Team

"*Healthy Rhythms for Leaders* is the resource that every leader needs right now. With accessible content and a practical format, this book is a tool that will help leaders establish or re-establish healthy rhythms."

— **Wesley Bolden**, Stadia Church Planting

"*Healthy Rhythms for Leaders* is a wonderfully accessible and very timely resource for those interested in growing and helping others grow in ministry. Standing on a strong foundation of Scripture and theological reflection, Winfield and Mark help us rediscover a missional spirituality that is badly needed to address the complexities of ministry in our current climate. You will not be disappointed!"

— **Kimberly D. Reisman**, Executive Director,
World Methodist Evangelism

"*Healthy Rhythms for Leaders* is a wonderful gift from seasoned leaders Winfield Bevins and Mark Dunwoody. This is a wise and insightful book that will help missional leaders not just survive but thrive!"

— **Matthew Porter**, Leader of The Belfrey in York, UK
and Author of *A–Z of Prayer*

"This book offers leaders an integrative vision for the Christian life—of both worship and mission, advance and retreat, working and waiting. But it goes further by providing a practical application process to learning and sharing it with others. This book is well-worth reading—but best practiced."

— **Manik Corea**, Global Executive, New Anglican
Missionary Society (NAMS) and Regional Team Leader for
South-East Asia

"Melding ancient traditional spirituality with current contemporary lifestyles, the authors seek to safeguard, protect, and nurture leaders. This is an important and often neglected area, not readily found in current literature. As we deal with so many challenges in the world, it is essential that we internalize the teachings found in this book. This is a must read!"

— **Paul Siaki**, Missionary, Johannesburg, South Africa
and Author of *Becoming Church Unusual*

"In *Healthy Rhythms for Leaders*, Winfield Bevins and Mark Dunwoody introduce us to a unique model that weds spiritual practices with missional practices. This book equips leaders by connecting common principles and practices from the past to the present, in order to propel leaders for the fulfillment and completion of the Great Commission."

— **Will Plitt**, Executive Director Christ Together

HEALTHY RHYTHMS FOR LEADERS

Cultivating Soul Care

in Uncertain Times

AN EXPONENTIAL SERIES RESOURCE

Winfield Bevins & Mark Dunwoody

☰XPONENTIAL˥

Healthy Rhythms for Leaders: Cultivating Soul Care in Uncertain Times
Copyright © 2021 by Winfield Bevins and Mark Dunwoody

Exponential is a growing movement of activists committed to the multiplication of healthy new churches. Exponential Resources spotlights actionable principles, ideas and solutions for the accelerated multiplication of healthy, reproducing faith communities. For more information, visit exponential.org.

This book is manufactured in the United States.

ISBN 13-978-1-62424-057-7 (ebook)
ISBN 13- 978-1-62424-058-4 (print)

Cover and interior design by Harrington Interactive Media (harringtoninteractive.com)

≡XPONENTIAL⌐
RESOURCING CHURCH PLANTERS

- 90+ eBooks
- Largest annual church planting conference in the world (Exponential Global Event in Orlando)
- Regional Conferences - Boise, DC, Southern CA, Bay Area CA, Chicago, Houston and New York City
- Exponential Español (spoken in Spanish)
- 200+ Roundtables on Topics like Church Multiplication, Mobilization, Church Planting, Emotionally Healthy Leaders, The Future of the Church, and More
- Exponential HUB - Free Digital Platform offering content & conversation (multiplication.org/HUB)
- FREE Online Multiplication & Mobilization Assessments
- FREE Online Multiplication & Mobilization Courses
- Conference content available via Digital Access Pass (Training Videos)
- Weekly Newsletter
- 1000+ Hours of Free Audio Training
- 100s of Hours of Free Video Training
- Free Podcast Interviews

exponential.org

Twitter.com/churchplanting
Facebook.com/churchplanting
Instagram.com/church_planting

THE INVITATION

"Are you tired?
Worn out?
Burned out on religion?
Come to me.
Get away with me and you'll recover your life.
I'll show you how to take a real rest.
Walk with me and work with me—watch how I do it.
Learn the unforced rhythms of grace.
I won't lay anything heavy or ill-fitting on you.
Keep company with me and
you'll learn to live freely and lightly."

— Jesus Christ
Matthew 11:28–30, *The Message*

INSIDE

TWO FRIENDS, ONE PILGRIMAGE

We wrote this book as friends: an Irishman (Mark) and an American (Winfield). Together, we have more than four decades of experience training and coaching leaders from around the world. We have trained leaders and worked with organizations that have started hundreds of new churches and fresh expressions of church in a wide variety of contexts around the world. These experiences show that we are no armchair theologians. Having worked with hundreds of leaders (not to mention our personal ministry experiences), we also know that life and ministry are difficult and can be unbearable at times, especially if our lives are not rooted in a deep spirituality. More than ever before, leaders need soul care.

A few years ago, we shared a lifechanging pilgrimage together in Northern England, traveling to the ruins of Whitby Abbey, to the Durham Cathedral, and to the island of Lindisfarne, where we ended with a retreat. On Lindisfarne Island, we were both deeply moved by the life and legacy of St. Aidan, who came from Iona in the seventh century to evangelize northern England. Aidan and the monks of Lindisfarne embodied a deep missional spirituality, which we have begun to call an "ebb and flow way of life." This way of life was marked by outreach and withdrawal, worship, prayer, and mission. As we walked around the island and prayed, we got a sense that rediscovering this way of missional living is essential for leaders in today's world.

Since our retreat on Lindisfarne Island, we have both felt an overwhelming need to share with others what we learned during that trip and what we've learned since that time. That's why we have written this book to help leaders cultivate soul care that connects spiritual practices with missional practices to promote healthy rhythms in their life, as well as for those the lead. Although much of what we have written is based on ancient practices, we believe that this framework can help missional leaders thrive in today's globally diverse world. We pray this book will offer a helpful introduction to healthy rhythms for leaders that will encourage and equip you to fulfill God's mission wherever God might call you to serve.

— Winfield Bevins & Mark Dunwoody

DISCOVER A NEW BEACH

"There will be no new normal. We are now dealing with a world that is going to be ferocious. The volatilities, the turbulence, the uncertainties of the world will probably define the second half of my life."
— JIM COLLINS

W e live in a strange world, where things like pandemics and protests seem to be the new norm. Since March 2020, when the COVID-19 pandemic began to settle in, the world has radically changed and will continue to change in the days ahead. Andy Crouch, Kurt Keilhacker, and Dave Blanchard describe the effects of this global pandemic as an economic and cultural blizzard, winter, and the beginning of a "little ice age—a once-in-a-lifetime change that is likely to affect our lives and organizations for years."[1] One thing is for certain; we live in a different world than before, and things may never return to the way they were.

At the time of writing this (during the COVID-19 pandemic), daily news is filled with extreme changes, and many of us feel battered by forces we cannot control. Yet many leaders are still using old maps for a world that no longer exists. We cannot hope to make sense of our new world by using old maps. It doesn't help to dust them off or reprint them with bolder colors. The more we rely on them, the more confused we will become. They will cause us to focus on the wrong things and blind us to what's significant. Continuing to use maps that helped make sense of our previous world will only lead to greater confusion. We need a new GPS to navigate the realities of the new world in which we now live.

Strangely, I (Mark) have always been intrigued and excited by times of change and chaos. Living next to the ocean in beautiful Ireland, I have always marveled at the intense Atlantic Ocean storms that frequently battered the exposed coast. Storms can dramatically change how a beach looks because they often cause erosion and other shoreline changes from high winds and waves.

We need to discover "new beaches," where God has gone before us to create beauty and wonder.

During that season of life, I would walk down to the waterfront after a storm had passed, not to look at the damage, eroded shorelines, or fallen trees—but to find a new beach. Such are the times we are living in today. The world has changed, and we need to discover "new beaches," where God has gone before us to create beauty and wonder.

We know the relationship between the church and mission has always been a complex one. Ask three Christian leaders about this topic and get three different answers. While it is true that the church was founded in mission, it is also true that the stronger the church grew, the more mission became only one item on a very long agenda. Whatever your personal beliefs, hopes, and dreams for the Church, we invite you to consider that we need new rhythms to help navigate this chaotic time.

We also know life is hard and you might have been disappointed by the church's response to, or feel lost in, the current state of global pandemic. Truth be told, many leaders find themselves at a loss in times of crisis, and are still firmly in a mode of "doing" by creating more programs and activities. The pandemic has likely resulted in many leaders duplicating this busyness in an online format—while unwittingly neglecting their spiritual rhythm of life.

Yet, Scripture and church history prove that even in times of crisis and pain, hope can emerge. The key to seeing hope's emergence is for us to be aware of God's presence in every part of our lives because that awareness guides us to a place of missional creativity. We passionately believe it is critical for leaders to embrace for themselves spiritual formation that is grounded in the hope of Christ.

With lives that have been marked by hurry and distraction, church leaders are in desperate need of balancing themselves again if they are ever to sustain a missional lifestyle. In the midst of our world's radical changes and challenges, we need courageous leaders who are willing to take time to care for their souls—and the souls of others.

ABOUT THE BOOK

We want to invite you as a leader on a journey to slow down and care for your soul. In our work with leaders, we call this "soul care for leaders," which means tending to the inner spiritual life of a leader. As leaders, we too often focus on external things like vision-casting, strategic planning, busy work, and countless meetings—all at the neglect of our own souls. However, Jesus warns us, "What good is it for someone to gain the whole world, yet forfeit their soul?" (Mark 8:36). These words still ring true more than 2,000 years later. Dallas Willard describes soul in the following way:

> It includes an individual's thoughts and feelings, along with heart or will, with its intents and choices. It also includes an individual's bodily life and social relations, which, in their inner meaning and nature, are just as 'hidden' as the thoughts and feelings. The secret to a strong, healthy, and fruitful ministerial life lies in how we work *with* God in all of these dimensions. Together they make up the real person . . . . The inner dimensions of life are what are referred to in the Great Commandment: 'Love the Lord your God with all your heart, and with all your soul, and with all your strength, and with all your mind; and your neighbor as yourself' (Luke 10:27, NASB). This commandment does not so much tell us what we must do, as what we must cultivate in the care of our souls.[2]

Here Willard tells us that soul care is tending to the inner dimension of the soul, which we too often neglect. In this book, we define soul care as simply taking time to cultivate the inner spiritual life through practicing healthy rhythms. Throughout the book, we use "soul care" and "spiritual formation" interchangeably because they both deal with tending to our inner spiritual life.

We believe that one of the primary ways we can practice soul care is by establishing healthy rhythms, which we use synonymously with "spiritual disciplines." Healthy rhythms are essentially holy habits that root us in the life of God. The recovery of a disciplined or rhythmic life is in keeping with the apostle Paul's words to his young apprentice: "Discipline yourself for the purpose of godliness" (1 Tim. 4:7, NASB). The word discipline, which is derived from the Greek word *gumnasia* (from which we get our word "gymnasium"), literally means "exercise." As we engage in spiritual disciplines, it's like we are essentially exercising the inner life of the soul. That is, just as physical exercise promotes strength in the body, the spiritual disciplines promote soul care and growth in grace. Healthy rhythms provide a pathway through which the grace of God transforms us from the inside out and makes us increasingly like Jesus.

Throughout the book, we draw from rich a Christian tradition of spiritual formation and soul care that is rooted in the Scriptures and can be found running throughout the pages of church history. The voices of spiritual formation and soul care from which we draw are diverse and include Christians from all ages. For instance, in a recent book entitled *Soul Care in African American Practice*, Barbara L. Peacock reminds us that regardless of one's ethnicity, the practices of prayer, spiritual direction, and soul care are disciplines that promote

- A more intimate relationship with God,
- Increased discipline,
- Greater conviction in one's prayer life,
- Greater sensitivity to the presence of God,
- The transformation of one's personal and public life, and
- Power to live out the resurrected life on a daily basis.[3]

In the following pages, you will be introduced to various practices and voices from the ages. Although much of what we share in this book is founded on ancient practices, we believe that these rhythms can help leaders thrive in today's globally diverse world. We believe that the practices in this book can be adapted to different contexts.

We have written *Healthy Rhythms for Leaders* primarily to help Christian leaders care for their own souls in today's chaotic and uncertain world. It is designed to help all types of leaders—whether they be healthcare workers, business owners, pastors, community leaders, or church planters—to go deeper in their own personal faith and walk with Christ. It is also intended to help leaders share these practices and principles with those they serve in their churches and organizations.

We have divided the book into three sections, which represent movements of thought. When taken together, we believe these three movements will help you and those you serve navigate our changing world. The first movement is *personal rhythms*, which focus on the inner life of a leader. Nothing could be more important or more needed in today's uncertain world than developing our inner life with God. That's why Part One focuses on developing healthy spiritual rhythms in your life, which includes chapters on spiritual breathing, developing a rule a life, and cultivating the art of spiritual reflection.

The second movement (Part Two) is *leadership rhythms*, which refers to our outer life. This section includes practices that will help your leadership navigate the chaotic and uncertain world. This includes chapters on leadership essentials for today that is based on our study of leadership resilience and on cultivating missional innovation through the lens of "Design Thinking."

The third movement (Part Three) is *corporate rhythms*, which remind us of our life together. This part includes chapters on becoming a spiritual guide for others and starting "Soul Care Groups."

Once you've finished these three parts, the remainder of the book offers various tools you can use to implement the practices from this book into real life. We hope that the overall structure will assist you as you seek to put into practice healthy rhythms wherever you led. Each chapter ends with a prayer that we have either written or drawn from others that will help you reflect on the theme of the contents.

Whoever you are, wherever you are, we are all called to be emotionally and spiritually healthy leaders who proclaim the life-giving gospel of Jesus Christ afresh to our generation. Let's begin the journey!

We are all called to be emotionally and spiritualty healthy leaders

Part One

PERSONAL RHYTHMS

Chapter 1

DEVELOPING SPIRITUAL BREATHING

"One of the most important rhythms for a person in ministry is to establish a constant back-and-forth motion between engagement and retreat."

— RUTH HALEY BARTON

We invite you to take a journey with us to rediscover the rhythms of missional spirituality.

All around the world, many leaders are running on empty, on the verge of burnout, and suffering from "SADD": Spiritual Attention Deficit Disorder. One of the reasons for this is that many leaders are trying to serve God in our own power and strength. Mission without prayer and worship is dangerous, though, and disembodied too. Oftentimes, we falsely divorce missional practices from spiritual practices, as if mission was something non-spiritual and merely pragmatic, dependent upon us—not on God. Could anything be further from the truth? If mission is anything, shouldn't it be spiritual and influenced by the Spirit of the living God, rather

> *If mission is anything, shouldn't it be spiritual and influenced by the Spirit of the living God?*

than something we attempt in our own strength and power? No wonder so many Christians are departing from the faith.

Perhaps you are at the point of burnout or have a close friend or associate who is there. Author Henri Nouwen describes his own experience after more than twenty years of ministry. Read closely his words:

> I found myself praying poorly, living somewhat isolated from other people, and very much preoccupied with burning issues. Everyone was saying that I was doing really well, but something inside was telling me that my success was putting my own soul in danger. I began to ask whether my lack of contemplative prayer, my loneliness, and my constantly changing involvement in what seemed most urgent were signs that the Spirit was gradually being suppressed. It was very hard for me to see clearly, and though I never spoke hell or only jokingly so, I woke up one day with the realization that I was living in a very dark place and that the term "burnout" was a convenient psychological translation for spiritual death.[4]

I (Winfield) remember the first time I read these words because they hit a little too close to home. For too many leaders today, these words are daily realities. But it doesn't have to be this way.

We believe that Christian leaders need to rediscover holistic practices for spiritual formation that will sustain them for mission in today's world. Christianity is not just a set of doctrines to be affirmed but a way of life that is meant to be lived. The earliest Christians were simply known by their association with "the Way" (Acts 9:2; 18:25; 22:4; 24:14).

They were associated with "the Way" because they followed the way of Jesus. We need to rediscover this ancient way of being a Christian that brings together worship, formation, and mission—which we call "missional spirituality" because it connects spiritual practices with missional practices.

Just as breathing is essential to the physical body, so the Christian life requires spiritual breathing. Breathing is a beautiful analogy for the Christian life because it reminds us that our mission is directly connected to our spirituality. Let us explain. Mission isn't just doing something *for* God; it begins and ends with being *with* God. In their book, *Worship and Mission After Christendom*, Alan and Eleanor Kreider say the Church needs to both inhale in worship and exhale by going into the world and sharing the Good News; making peace; and caring for creation, reconciliation, and the marginalized of society.[5] In missional spirituality, "inhaling" and "exhaling" are two essential and interconnected movements of living the way of Jesus in the world.

This balance of worship and mission is especially important for missional leaders today. Even activities like ministry and mission can be a distraction if we don't allow time for rest. After the disciples returned from a busy missionary journey, Jesus told them, "Come aside by yourselves to a deserted place and rest awhile" (Mark 6:31). They had been busy and Jesus knew that they needed rest for their weary souls. Spiritual burnout occurs when we don't give ourselves time to rest from our daily routine. We believe that the secret of Jesus' ministry can be found in this balance of worship, prayer, and mission. Henri Nouwen offers addition insight with the following meditation on the balance of the spiritual life and ministry of Jesus.

"In the morning, long before dawn, he got up and left the house, and went off to a lonely place and prayed there." In the middle of sentences loaded with action—healing suffering people, casting out devils, responding to impatient disciples, traveling from town to town and preaching from synagogue to synagogue—we find these quiet words: "In the morning, long before dawn, he got up and left the house, and went off to a lonely place and prayed there." In the center of breathless activities we hear a restful breathing. Surrounded by hours of moving we find a moment of quiet stillness. In the heart of much involvement there are words of withdrawal. In the midst of action there is contemplation. And after much togetherness there is solitude. The more I read this nearly silent sentence locked in between the loud words of action, the more I have the sense that the secret of Jesus's ministry is hidden in that lonely place where he went to pray, early in the morning, long before dawn.[6]

We also see the importance of rest illustrated in the story of Mary and Martha in Luke 10:38–42. Mary sat at the feet of Jesus and heard his word, but Martha was distracted with much serving. Jesus said that Mary had chosen the best thing because she sat at his feet and was not distracted. Resting in the Lord is the only way that we can continue to have an effective Christian life because our *being* must come before our *doing.* Times of rest and retreat enable us to listen to the still small voice of God.

Several years ago, I (Winfield) went through a difficult season wherein I felt spiritually exhausted and close to ministry burnout. Like Bilbo Baggins in *The Fellowship of the Ring,* I felt "thin, sort of *stretched,* like butter scraped over too much bread."[7] My faith had not adequately prepared me for that experience. During that season of life, God helped me slow down and recover my faith by embracing spiritual rest and retreat. Jesus invites each one of us to come and find our rest in him. Take a moment and reflect on the following words from Matthew's Gospel:

> Are you tired? Worn out? Burned out on religion? Come to me. Get away with me and you'll recover your life. I'll show you how to take a real rest. Walk with me and work with me—watch how I do it. Learn the unforced rhythms of grace. I won't lay anything heavy or ill-fitting on you. Keep company with me and you'll learn to live freely and lightly. (Matthew 11:28–30, MSG)

Never before has there been such a need to rediscover missional spirituality. It is essential that we allow time during each day for spiritual rest and solitude from all of the busy distractions of our complex world. If we are not careful, the distractions of this world will keep us from finding rest for our souls. Our souls need to have rest in the same way that our physical bodies need rest; otherwise, we will experience spiritual burnout. God promises rest to his people. The biblical Greek word for rest literally means a resting place, a quiet place, peace, trust, and reliance. Rest is the reason why God commanded us to keep the Sabbath. Jesus said that the Sabbath was created so that man may have rest (Mark 2:27). As we shall see in the next section, rest and mission are not antithetical to one another, but instead work together symbiotically.

The biblical Greek word for rest literally means a resting place, a quiet place, peace, trust, and reliance.

THE MISSIONAL SPIRITUALITY OF LINDISFARNE

Sometimes, we have to go a long way to find what we are looking for. One of the best examples of missional spirituality comes to us from a tiny island in northern England. Lindisfarne Island, which we mentioned in the preface, is the site of one of the most important centers of early Christianity in England. Over the ages, it has been home to saints and scholars, including St. Aidan and St. Cuthbert. It also famously produced the medieval illuminated texts known as the *Lindisfarne Gospel,* an artistic masterpiece. From the shores of this island, missionary monks spread the gospel like wildfire across northern England. Today, the island's history, beauty, and wonder continue to inspire a new generation for mission. So what can a body of land that only measures three miles from its east coast to its west coast teach us about doing mission today? We believe that the missional spirituality of Lindisfarne Island still has many lessons to teach us.

In 633 A.D., King Oswald of Northumbria desired to bring Christianity to his kingdom and requested the monks of Iona, Scotland, to come and bring Christianity to his people. Corman, the first monk sent from Iona was met with little success. He returned to Iona and reported he was unable to minister to the people because they "were ungovernable and of an obstinate and barbarous temperament."[8] Not willing to give up, the monks of Iona had a conference to discuss what they should do next. Aidan, who was at the conference, issued these comments to the failed missionary monk:

> Brother, it seems to me that you were too severe on your ignorant hearers. You should have followed the practice of

> the Apostles, and begun by giving them the milk of simpler
> teaching, and gradually nourished them with the word of
> God until they were capable of greater perfection and able
> to follow the loftier precepts of Christ.[9]

This observation by St. Aidan convinced all in attendance
that he was the man to continue the failed missionary work
in Northumbria. They unanimously decided that Aidan
would be sent out from Iona to establish Christianity in
northern England.

Aidan was consecrated a bishop and arrived in Northumbria
around 635 A.D. accompanied by twelve other monks. King
Oswald gave him the small island of Lindisfarne (also known
as Holy Island) as a home base for his monastic work. Aidan
established the monastery on the Island of Lindisfarne that
eventually became an epicenter for spirituality and mission for
northern England.

The landscape of Lindisfarne Island is littered with
monuments, markings, and ruins that once boldly stated, "This
is a thin place. This is holy ground." During our last visit,
Winfield and I (Mark) looked at each other and asked if we
both sensed that the very ground itself seemed to be calling out,
"Come here and be transformed." In moments such as those,
visitors to the island today can feel the connection with the
people whose spirits first marked these spots and all the pilgrims
who have since visited.

Lindisfarne provided the monks both solitude and a base
for missionary work, being cut off from the mainland, except
for twice a day during low tide. When the tide was in, the
island was completely surrounded by water and became a
solitary place. When the tide went out, it again was connected

to the mainland. This rhythm of the tides coming in and going out formed the spiritual rhythms of the missionary monks on Lindisfarne. The monks would retreat on the island for worship, prayer, and rest, and then carry God's presence back out into mission. Lindisfarne became a center of learning to train missionary monks for Northumbria and eventually helped found other monasteries throughout the region.[10]

What made Lindisfarne such a successful missionary hub? We believe that it was due to the missional spirituality of its leader, St. Aidan, who was a humble man of God with a deep spirituality that included a life of prayer, reading the Scriptures, and proclaiming Christ in word and deed. Aidan, whose name means "little flame," lit a fire that burned brightly across Northern England. The ancient historian Bede described him as a "man of outstanding gentleness, holiness, and moderation," who was endowed with the "grace of discretion."[11] In addition to living a holy life, he gave his clergy "an inspiring example of self-discipline and continence," never caring about worldly possessions, and he also loved to give to the poor.[12] Aidan refused to use the king of Northumbria's horse for his missionary journeys, but instead chose to travel on foot, reading the Scriptures and talking about God to everyone he met. He preached widely throughout Northumbria, working together with the king to evangelize the people. Bede summarized Aidan's life in the following words:

> He cultivated peace and love, purity and humility; he was above anger and greed, and desired pride and conceit; he set himself to keep as well as to teach the laws of God, and was diligent in study and prayer. He used his priestly authority to check the proud and powerful; he tenderly comforted the

sick; he relieved and protected the poor. To sum up in brief what I have learned from those who knew him, he took pains never to neglect anything that he had learned from the writings of the evangelists, apostles, and prophets, and he set himself to carry them out with all his powers.[13]

Such was the spiritual life of Aiden of Lindisfarne. Ray Simpson reminds us, "The pattern of outreach and withdrawal, advance and retreat, was another feature of Aidan's, as of Christ's, way of life."[14] The monks of Lindisfarne carried God with them far

> *Missional spirituality is marked by the ebb and flow of the Christian life.*

and wide out of a deep place of rest and delight in God's presence. Missional spirituality is marked by the ebb and flow of the Christian life. So it should be with us; our mission to the world should flow from a deep well within us, from the very presence of the living God. These practices form the heart of missional spirituality.

The ultimate fruit of spiritual formation is not retreat from the world, but missional engagement with the world. Robert Mulholland reminds us: "Spiritual formation is a process of being conformed to the image of Christ for the sake of others."[15] This definition of spiritual formation reminds us that the *telos*, or goal, of our own formation as leaders is not just for ourselves, but for the sake of others. To be a Christian leader is to be a part of a missionary movement that has a long and rich heritage of holistic mission. This heritage reminds us that God's love inspires us to be missionaries to the world around us. Many Christians around the world have adopted the "Five Marks of Mission," which is a commitment to, and understanding of, God's holistic and integral mission.[16] We believe that these five marks offer the Church a holistic model of mission for the twenty-first century. The Five Marks of Mission are:

1. To proclaim the Good News of the kingdom
2. To teach, baptize, and nurture new believers
3. To respond to human need by loving service
4. To transform unjust structures of society and challenge violence of every kind while pursuing peace and reconciliation
5. To strive to safeguard the integrity of creation and sustain and renew the life of the earth.

Every Christian, regardless of tradition or background, can be missional by joining in God's mission through these marks. Whether we're proclaiming the gospel in word and deed, making disciples, serving the needs of others, pursuing peace and reconciliation, or taking care of creation, we can all share in the responsibility of fulfilling God's mission on the earth.

In conclusion, God's love inspires us all to be missionaries to the world around us. As N. T. Wright says, "The link between worship and mission is so close that many prefer to speak of them in terms of each other. Glad, rich worship of God revealed in Jesus invites outsiders to come in, welcomes them, nourishes them, and challenges them . . . . Thus, though I continue to speak of worship and mission as separate activities, I also insist on integrating them."[17] As members of the body of Christ, we come together to worship God *in order to be sent back out into the world through mission.* Let's end this chapter with a prayer attributed to St. Aidan, which embodies the rhythms of missional spirituality.

CLOSING PRAYER

Leave me alone with God as much as may be.
As the tide draws the waters close in upon the shore,
Make me an island, set apart,
Alone with you, God, holy to you.
Then with the turning of the tide,
Prepare me to carry your presence to the busy world beyond,
The world that rushes in on me,
Till the waters come again and fold me back to you.
— St. Aidan

ESSENTIAL THOUGHT FROM THE CHAPTER

Spiritual breathing is a way of Christian living that connects spiritual practices with missional practices and reminds us that our mission to the world should flow from the very presence of the living God.

Practice

Take at least half a day for personal spiritual retreat to reflect on developing a more robust missional spirituality in your life. Bring a Bible and a journal with you to reflect on how you can develop a deeper missional spirituality that includes the balance of your spiritual breathing: worship and mission.

Chapter 2

EBB AND FLOW RULE OF LIFE

"Your personal rule of life is a holistic description of the Spirit-empowered rhythms and relationships that create, redeem, sustain and transform the life God invites you to humbly fulfill for Christ's glory."
— STEPHEN A. MACCHIA

I f you think about it, we are creatures of habit. We have rhythms, routines, and rituals that make up our daily lives, and for many of us, these routines maintain our sanity. We might wake up in the morning, drink a cup of coffee, brush our teeth, and read the news. Or maybe we start the day off with a simple prayer and Bible reading. Routines and rituals like these can be good things!

We all need spiritual rhythms for our daily lives, whatever those practices might be. One of the biggest challenges for most people is that their rhythms have been disrupted by the recent pandemic. Many people are working from home, homeschooling their children, and practically living on Zoom. Our old rhythms no longer work in a new world. We need to find new rhythms for our lives.

There exists a timeless Christian practice of regulating our daily practices and rhythms called a "rule of Life." Maybe you are wondering, *What is a Rule of Life?* It serves as a framework for freedom: not as a set of rules that restrict or deny life, but as a way of living out our vocations both individually and together. It is rooted in Scripture, always pointing to Christ. Think of your Rule of Life like a trellis for your faith. With a trellis for structure, fruit can grow. Jesus talks about the importance of having a deep and abiding relationship with God—"abiding with him" (John 15:4–8). Even with all of our skills and talents, we can't do anything unless it is in partnership with God. Of course, fruit from the vine can still grow on the ground, but it will rot unless it can reach up to the sun. Likewise, we need a framework to help us reach up to God.

A modern example of a rule of life is one that Martin Luther King Jr. created to guide nonviolent protests of the civil rights movement. His rule emphasized daily spiritual principles and practices that were designed to sustain the social action of the movement. Things like prayer, meditation, service, and non-violence were at the heart of his rule that every demonstrator had to agree with:

- Meditate daily on the teachings and life of Jesus.
- Remember always that the nonviolent movement in Birmingham seeks justice and reconciliation—not victory.
- Walk and talk in the manner of love, for God is love.
- Pray daily to be used by God in order that all men might be free.
- Sacrifice personal wishes in order that all men might be free.
- Observe with both friend and foe the ordinary rules of courtesy.
- Seek to perform regular service for others and for the world.

- Refrain from the violence of fist, tongue, or heart.
- Strive to be in good spiritual and bodily health.
- Follow the directions of the movement and of the captain on a demonstration.[18]

Having a personal rule of life helps us abide with Christ in our everyday lives. The purpose of our abiding with God is that we can bear fruit in the world; it is not just to have warm, fuzzy feelings or to wait to go to heaven. Fruit can't do anything unless it's attached to the vine (John 15:4); similarly, without God, we can't do anything. In Philippians 4:7, Paul talks about a profound relationship of total abandonment that surpasses understanding (e.g., God abandons himself to love us). How, then, can we know something that "surpasses understanding"? Paul is talking about an experiential relationship that surpasses all *cognitive* understanding. Christianity is not merely a moral code, but involves a direct sharing in divine life with our Creator.

How is the world going to believe in Jesus? They won't believe unless they see him abiding in us. And they won't see him in us unless we are abiding in him: a Christ-centered life lived out of a holy center that comes from a holy concern for the world. Second Corinthians 4:16 says, "Though outwardly we are wasting away, yet inwardly we are being renewed day by day." God prunes the vines that produce fruit; God will prune anything out of our life that is not Christlike. There is a type of growth that mimics healthy growth called "sucker growth." These branches look great and even turn a wonderful color. However, God will prune things out of our lives that, while they may appear good, provide little value to us.

Part of the pruning God wants to do in our lives happens through silence, solitude, and stillness. The Psalms remind us to "be still, and know that I am God" (Ps. 46:10). We must develop in our spiritual lives daily disciplines of spiritual practices to dwell in God's presence. We need to learn to spend time every day being still with God because without being centered in God, there is nothing for him that you and I can do.

> *Part of the pruning God wants to do in our lives happens through silence, solitude, and stillness.*

THE RHYTHMS OF EBB AND FLOW

Remember the missional spirituality of the monks of Lindisfarne Island that we discussed in Chapter 1? The legacy of Aidan reminds us that just like the analogy of breathing—inhaling and exhaling—the tides remind us of the ebb and flow of the spiritual life. Ebb refers to the outgoing tide, when the water drains away from the shore; flow refers to the incoming tide, when the water rises again.

We can see a similar pattern of ebb and flow in the life of one of our heroes, Desmond Tutu, who was a South African Anglican archbishop known for his opposition to apartheid in South Africa. His work against apartheid earned him the Nobel Prize for Peace in 1984 in recognition of "the courage and heroism shown by black South Africans in their time with the peaceful method of struggle against apartheid." He brought incredible courage and spiritual leadership to the movement that overturned apartheid. The following quote demonstrates his ebb and flow—a balance of healthy rhythms—that sustained his daily life and ministry.

People often ask about the source of my joy, and I can honestly say that it comes from my spiritual life and specifically it comes from times of stillness. They are indispensable part of my day regardless of what else I might face. I pray out loud or to myself before every meeting, and before every drive in the car. I also take quiet days when I do not talk—at least until supper. Once a month I take a room at a local convent and spend a day sleeping, eating, praying, and reading, and at least once a year I go on a retreat of three or more days. The importance of these retreats is hard to convey-through them I am strengthened and am able to hear what God is saying and to seek solutions to problems that seem unsolvable.[19]

Rhythms of ebb and flow like this can be a powerful example for us as we seek to develop what we're calling an "Ebb and Flow Rule of Life." Rhythms of ebb and flow aren't just meant to be occasional or haphazard. We need to develop daily, weekly, monthly, and annual rhythms of ebb and flow to sustain the life of a missional leader.

Daily. There are four areas to think about applying rhythms of life. The first is daily. Each day should be planned out to promote a balance of prayer, rest, work, recreation, and outreach. Prioritize what matters most each day. I (Winfield) start the day with a cup of coffee, prayer, and Bible study— usually in that order! I begin working around 9 a.m., take a break for lunch and work until mid-afternoon and take time for tea in the afternoon around 3 p.m. This allows me to pause for prayer and reflection before I finish the day.

Weekly. Most of us live from week to week. If we are not careful we will lose the importance of having specific days for rest and reflection. It is essential for Christian leaders to have a day off for Sabbath rest. Sadly, church leaders often work on Sundays and as a consequence don't take time off. Whatever the day is, schedule a Sabbath day off for rest, renewal, and reflection. For me (Winfield), Friday nights are family night and Saturdays are for fun and recreation. Whatever your week looks like, schedule days for what matters most.

Monthly. The months of the year can remind us of the importance of seasons of life. Each season brings its own unique rhythm, weather, traditions, and memories. Spring, summer, fall, and winter can be powerful reminders of the seasons and rhythms of the spiritual life. The Christian life has different seasons just as the seasons of nature. Each of these seasons remind us of the multidimensional nature of discipleship. For instance, some months are better to plan extended time off for pray, retreat, and recreation—like summer or fall. Spring is often a busy time when people get back to work after the long winter. Plan out your months to include days and even weeks for time to live out rhythms of grace.

Annually. Finally, as you plan out the year, make sure that you build in annual rhythms that encourage emotional and spiritual health. Schedule things like holidays and retreats. One of the things that we have come to realize is that if you don't schedule time off it will never happen. Often times we keep putting things off that we know we should do. Regular times of rest and retreat should be scheduled so that we will not forget them in the busyness of life.

David Cole of the Community of Aidan and Hilda has written extensively on the life of prayer and how it connects to mission. He offers the following suggestions for creating a regular practice of rest and retreat in your everyday life that we have found helpful.

1. Meditate momentarily: take time throughout the day to do this.
2. Divert daily: focus attention on the Bible or other meditation.
3. Withdraw weekly: for an hour or two of silence.
4. Make a date monthly: for a day devoted to God alone.
5. Abdicate annually: go to a monastery, retreat house, or desert.[20]

When developing a Rule of Life, the key is to keep it simple! It should include personal spiritual disciplines and practices that apply to your personal life, your family life, your ministry life, your community life, and your global commitment. Spiritual disciplines are essentially holy habits that root us in the life of God.

Author Steven Harper writes, "In our day and time we are witnessing a new emergence of the Spirit all over the earth and, along with it, a new commitment to the practice of the means of grace and the keeping of other spiritual disciplines."[21] Many Christians today are discovering that spiritual disciplines have been passed like a baton from biblical times through the ages of church history. They are still essential for spiritual formation for leaders today.

Christians today are discovering that spiritual disciplines have been passed like a baton from biblical times

We appreciate Richard Foster's list of disciplines in his book *Celebration of Discipline*, which explores the classic spiritual practices of the Christian faith.[22] Along the way, Foster shows that it is only by and through these practices that the true path to spiritual growth can be found. Dividing the disciplines into three movements of inward, outward, and corporate, Foster shows how each of these areas contribute to a balanced spiritual life. The inward Disciplines of meditation, prayer, fasting, and study, offer avenues of personal examination and change. The outward disciplines of simplicity, solitude, submission, and service, help prepare us to make the world a better place. The corporate disciplines of confession, worship, guidance, and celebration, bring us nearer to one another and to God.

We really like the way he divides the disciples into three movements, and as you develop your own rule of life, these can provide a helpful framework. We also like the following twelve spiritual disciplines that Peter Scazzero recommends in his book *Emotionally Healthy Spirituality.*[23] Here is a summary and suggestions that we have added to help you get started.

1. Scripture. It is essential to spend time in Scripture every day. You may begin by reading the Gospels or praying through the Psalms. You may also try reading the Bible through in a year or begin meditating on Scripture each day.

2. Silence and Solitude. We live a noisy world where we need to develop the practice of silence and solitude. You may want to take 10–20 minutes a day to be in stillness before the Lord or take a three-hour retreat once a month.

3. Daily (Office) Prayer. For centuries, Christian believers have employed a wonderful tool known as the Daily Office to help structure their prayers that includes fixed-hour prayers throughout the day. You may want to begin with having a designated time to pray rhythmically in the morning and evening over the next few months.

4. Study. We live in a technological world filled with screens where many people no longer take time to study or think for themselves. Don't forget about your mind! You may want to read a new book each month or take an online course.

5. Sabbath. We all desperately need Sabbath rest. You may want to begin setting apart a 24-hour period of Sabbath to the Lord each week if you do not do so already.

6. Simplicity. The world we are living in is filled with increasing complexity and anxiety. More than ever before we need the gift of simplicity. You may want to remove distractions by downsizing your commitments.

7. Play and Recreation. Take time off to rest and play! This may include finding activities that are life-giving, such as taking up a hobby like painting, hiking, cooking, or music.

8. Care for the Physical Body. God created us as holistic beings, with a mind, spirit, and body. Oftentimes, we don't take care of our bodies as we should. Healthy rhythms may include trying to get eight hours of sleep per night, exercising, or changing your diet.

9. Service and Mission. As Christians, we are called to reach out to the world around us in service and mission. It may be time for you to step out and share your faith and begin using your time and talents to serve others in your community.

10. Emotional Health. We can't be spiritually healthy without being emotionally healthy. The two are directly connected and interrelated. You may want to slow down, begin journaling, or even find a counselor for a season to help you become emotionally healthy.

11. Family. An important, yet too often neglected part of a leader's life is their family. This area focuses on growing in your marriage and parenting, or if you are single, growing in your relationships with others.

12. Community. God made us to live in community with others. Disciples are made in community, not isolation. You may want to join a small group or an accountability group, or again, find a mentor.

BRENÉ BROWN MEETS ST. BENEDICT

As we close out this chapter, we want to encourage you to take time to identify your own personal values so that you can live them out. According to the Oxford Dictionary, values are "principles or standards of behavior; one's judgement of what is important in life." The reality is that too often values end up being something that is written on a page, rather than lived in real life. If we want to live out our values, we have to take time to identify them. We both love the writings of Brené Brown, who is an author and research professor at the University of Houston. According to Dr. Brené Brown, "We can't live into values that we can't name."[24] This is why it is so important to know our values when crafting our rule of life. Brown also reminds us that, "Living into our values means that we do more than profess our values, we practice them."[25]

> *Too often values end up being something that is written on a page, rather than lived in real life.*

We have included a list of values in the back of this book that can help you get started. Take time to go through that list and identify your top two to three core values. We know it will be hard to only choose two or three; however, as Jim Collins says, "If you have more than three priorities, you have no priorities."[26] These values will help you prioritize the rhythms that you chose to put into your life. Then, after identifying your top two to three core values, spend time prayerfully creating a rule of life.

Stephen Macchia has written a very helpful book called Crafting a Rule of Life, in which he offers principles, biblical reflection, and historic insights that can help guide you as you craft a personal rule of life for yourself.[27] He suggests the following four things: First, *a Rule of Life needs to be Spirit-empowered*, which is best lived out under the guidance and empowerment of God's Spirit. Second, *a personal rule of life should include both rhythms and relationships* of life involving those around us. Third, *a rule of life is to be humbly fulfilled for Christ's glory*, not ours. Finally, he reminds us that *Christ is the ideal example of the embodiment of a personal rule of life*. In other words, the ultimate goal of a personal rule of life is Christ likeness, nothing more nothing less.

Following the structure of our book, we crafted a rule of life that is divided the rule of life into three categories: personal rhythms, leader's rhythms, and corporate rhythms. Take some time now on your own to pray over your Rule of Life and craft it in a manner that makes the most sense for your lifestyle. You can use Peter Scazzero's or Richard Foster's list of disciplines as you begin to develop your personal Rule of Life, which can be divided into the three movements of inward, outward, and corporate disciplines. There is sample Rule of Life worksheet in the back of this book that you can fill out to help you develop daily, weekly, monthly, and annual rhythms in your everyday life.

CLOSING PRAYER

Dear Lord, I realize that I cannot make it without you in my life.
As life ebbs and flows, guide me in the way that I should go.
Order my steps in your Word and help me establish healthy
rhythms in my life.
Come and assist my prayer life and empower me to be a witness for
Jesus Christ.
Help me share the message of faith in the power of your Spirit.
Give me a holy boldness to speak your words.
In the name of the Father, Son, and the Holy Spirit. Amen.

ESSENTIAL THOUGHT

An Ebb and Flow Rule of Life provides a framework for freedom—not as a set of rules that restrict or deny life, but as a way to help you develop daily, weekly, monthly, and annual rhythms of ebb and flow in your everyday life and ministry.

Practice

Set aside some time for prayerful reflection and start to write out an Ebb and Flow Rule of Life for your life. You and your context are unique and your rule of life should be unique to you as well. What rhythms do you want to adopt for daily, monthly, and annual practices?

Chapter 3

THE ART OF SPIRITUAL REFLECTION

"Among the practices that can help us attend to soul care at a basic level are solitude *and* silence. *We practice these by finding ways to be alone and away from talk and noise. We rest, we observe, we "smell the roses"—dare we say it?—we do* nothing."

– DALLAS WILLARD

We live in a busy world in which too many of us don't take the time to stop and reflect on what is happening in our lives, our families, and our world. Leaders are often men and women of action, but not too often men and women of contemplation and reflection. This results in stress, depression, and burnout. In a world filled with distractions, we need a quiet place to reflect and pray, one in which we can more easily hear God speak to us. Reflection is essential to the spiritual life and to missional formation. In this chapter, we explore three ways that you can develop the art of spiritual reflection: by spending time alone with God, by reflecting on the Word, and by using the Daily Examen.

TIME ALONE WITH GOD

We live in a world of noise, and with the abundance of messages we constantly encounter today, words have in many ways lost their meaning. We encounter messages in print, on signs, on billboards, on television and computer screens, and on our phones. We scan social media outlets and quickly read our emails and text messages. The average person is bombarded with over three-thousand advertising messages every day. One danger of living in this flood of messages is that the content drowns out the quiet voice of God. More than ever, we must learn to cultivate times of silence and solitude so we can slow down, reflect, and listen to the voice of God. This comes only as we create space in our busy lives for spending time alone with God.

There is no better way to develop this discipline than by pairing it with time alone in solitude. One result of making space for silence is that it attunes our ears to hear God's voice, who often speaks quietly. When we pause to experience silence, we can begin to value and appreciate the meaning of God's Word. Sadly, our prayers tend to be shallow, selfish, and lacking any serious reflection on the nature of God. We need prayers that arise from a deep place in our hearts, an experience of God, shaped by silence and solitude. These practices help us pray more thoughtfully as we stay focused on God and his kingdom.

All too often, we hear without truly *listening.* Times of silence enable us to listen to the still, small voice of God. We find this practice modeled by Jesus, who would often depart from the crowds after performing miracles and doing ministry. He spent periods of time in silence and solitude, alone with the Father. Consider the following Scriptures:

All too often, we hear without truly listening.

- "He went up on the mountain by Himself to pray. Now when evening came, He was alone there." (Matthew 14:23, NKJV)
- "He departed and went into a deserted place." (Luke 4:42, NKJV)
- "So He Himself *often* withdrew into the wilderness and prayed." (Luke 5:16, NKJV)
- "He went out to the mountain to pray, and continued all night in prayer." (Luke 6:12, NKJV)
- "He . . . went up on the mountain to pray." (Luke 9:28, NKJV)
- "He went out and departed to a solitary place; and there He prayed." (Mark 1:35, NKJV)
- "He departed to the mountain to pray." (Mark 6:46, NKJV)

We love these verses because they remind us that our Lord needed time to get away by himself to do nothing but pray and listen to the Father. It might sound cliché, but it is true: if Jesus were a proponent of this practice in his ancient time, perhaps it is something we should consider for our own lives today. We need to make space in our busy lives to reflect on what God is doing and listen to the voice of the Spirit.

Like Jesus, we need to find a deserted place to pause, reflect, and pray. The problem is many leaders are in a constant mode of "doing" as they create more programs and activities. Just as we decide to limit foods that aren't healthy for us, we must also choose to sometimes keep at bay the connectivity we are increasingly hardwired to adore. Likewise, the saints of the past reveal that quiet, contemplative prayer is something that can not only refresh us—physically, emotionally, physiologically, and spirituality—but also can transform our neighborhoods and our world. By living in the Spirit, we foster a spirituality that is not *just another connection* but rather the *connection* to the purposes of our lives.

We live in a world that works as hard as it can to banish silence from our everyday existence. Silence is the enemy of ease—and people want what's easy. It is seen as something to be avoided (a moment of awkwardness between conversations, for example), rather than something useful and valuable. Yet, many people today also yearn for the opportunity to step away from the noise and busyness of modern life and rediscover the potential of peace and quiet. In losing silence, we have lost something that can add value to our lives, both in our spiritual journey and in our psychological well-being.

We can trace this tension between listening and doing throughout church history. At a very human level, we all live out this tension of doing and being as we seek to love God, our neighbor, and ourselves. So what might it be about silence that both attracts and repels us? Maybe it is the emptiness it can bring, for silence takes away our distractions and leaves us with our selves—and of course, with God. In silence, there is no hiding place from the chatter of life. Silence offers space in which we are brought into an encounter with the Living God.

Silence takes away our distractions and leaves us with our selves.

REFLECTING ON THE SCRIPTURES

The second way of cultivating spiritual reflection in our lives is by taking time to reflect on the Scriptures. This is sometimes called *Lectio Divina*, which is a reflective way to read a passage of Scripture and pray at the same time. It reminds us that prayer and Bible study are inseparably linked and that Scripture should always be read in the context of prayer. Prayer is the medium through which we come into contact with the same Holy Spirit who inspired the authors of the Bible. As we read the Scriptures, the Spirit applies the truths of the Word to our hearts. Prayer is the necessary means whereby we understand the Word of God, because without the assistance of the Holy Spirit in prayer, we conduct our Bible study in vain.

Lectio Divina is an ancient form of spiritual reflection. Because prayer and studying the sacred Scriptures are important for growing in our faith, we enter into this exercise by immersing ourselves daily in the sacred texts. In Hebrew thought, meditating on Scripture means quietly repeating it, giving one's self entirely to God, and abandoning outside distractions. This understanding lies behind the meaning of the Hebrew word we commonly translate as "meditate." In Psalm 1:2, we are reminded to meditate on two things: the Word of God and the goodness of God. Paul affirms this when he writes to the Philippians, "Whatever things are true, whatever things *are* noble, whatever things *are* just, whatever things *are* pure, whatever things *are* lovely, whatever things *are* of good report . . . *meditate* on these things" (Phil. 4:8, NKJV). *Lectio Divina* is a practical, time-tested method of reading the Bible, and it has held a special place in the church through the centuries. It serves as a means of connecting with God through a personal experience of meditating on God's Word.

In a world filled with distractions, we need a quiet place where God can speak to us. Many people spend only a few minutes each day reading or meditating on the Bible, and often this isn't enough. We suggest starting with taking at least twenty minutes a day. Sitting and prayerfully meditating on

God's Word puts the cares of this world in proper perspective and opens us up to hear God speak to us. Unlike some other forms of meditation, *Lectio Divina* doesn't advocate emptying the mind. Instead, through this practice, we free our minds from distraction so that we can fill them with God's Word.

What does this look like? Simply choose a short passage of Scripture and prayerfully reflect on it, allowing it to sink into your heart and soul. Reflecting on the Scriptures reminds us that words matter to God; therefore, they should matter to us. God has ordained his Word to be a means of communion with him, and *Lectio Divina* helps us to clearly hear, reflect on, and respond to the God who spoke the world into existence.

THE DAILY EXAMEN

Another excellent way to practice the art of spiritual reflection comes from the life of Ignatius of Loyola who founded the Jesuit order in 1534. He wrote the *Spiritual Exercises* that explored a disciplined spiritual life that proposed ways to reflect upon and nourish a dedication to the love of God through prayer and devotion. The influence of St. Ignatius has continued throughout the ages, and is one of the best-known spiritual exercises today.

The beautiful rhythms of St. Ignatius' *Spiritual Exercise*s have deeply influenced many other Christian leaders both inside and outside the Church. One of these exercises is the ancient Daily Examen (also called the Ignatian Examen). St. Ignatius encouraged a practice of prayerful reflection on the events of the day to detect God's presence and to discern his direction for us. It adopts five steps, which are prayer for the Spirit's guidance, giving thanks for what is good, reviewing what is happening in your life, reflecting on what needs to happen, and resolving what to do next.

Although this practice is ancient in origin, many people today, both young and old, still use this simple reflective prayer. The Daily Examen can be practiced as a family, in a group, or by yourself. We suggest you find fifteen minutes during your daily routine to review the previous twenty-four hours of your life using this practice. Below is a sample version of the Examen.

1. RECENTER

Invite the Holy Spirit to come.

2. REJOICE

Look at your day in a spirit of gratitude.

3. REVIEW

Guided by the Holy Spirit, look back and review your day.

4. REFLECT

Acknowledge any sins, omissions, or shortcomings from your day.

5. RESOLVE

What do you need to do to respond?

We believe that creating space for time alone with God through solitude and silence, reflecting on the Scriptures, and practicing the Daily Examen are three crucial practices for missional leaders that will help in reflecting upon the important events of daily life and ministry. We also believe that together, these practices offer a holistic and reflective framework for coaching. In particular, the Daily Examen provides a reflective model to help us reflect daily (and even monthly) on what God is doing in our lives and ministries. We explore this connection to coaching more later in the book.

The ultimate goal of spiritual reflection is to help us respond

> *The ultimate goal of spiritual reflection is to help us respond faithfully to God's call.*

faithfully to God's call in every area of our lives. Time alone with God, spending time in the Word, daily reflection, and practical theology are essential practices that can help us stay rooted in God during challenging times.

We want to close this chapter with a beautiful meditation called "How good it is to center down" from Dr. Howard Thurman (1899–1981). Thurman was an African-American author, theologian, educator, and Civil Rights leader. As a prominent religious figure, he played a leading role in Civil Rights Movement of the twentieth century through his theology of nonviolence. He influenced leaders within the movement, including Martin Luther King, Jr., and he also served as Dean of Rankin Chapel at Howard University from 1932 to 1944, not to mention his service as Dean of Marsh Chapel at Boston University from 1953 to 1965. He wrote numerous books, including *Jesus and the Disinherited* (1949), *The Inward Journey* (1961), and *Disciplines of the Spirit* (1963). Take a few minutes to slowly reflect on his powerful words from *Meditations of the Heart*.

How good it is to center down!
To sit quietly and see one's self pass by!
The streets of our minds seethe with endless traffic;

Our spirits resound with clashings, with noisy silences,
While something deep within hungers and thirsts
for the still moment and the resting lull.
With full intensity we seek, ere the quiet
passes, a fresh sense of order in our living;
A direction, a strong sure purpose that will structure
our confusion and bring meaning in our chaos.
We look at ourselves in this waiting moment
—the kinds of people we are.
The questions persist: what are we doing with our lives?
—what are the motives that order our days?
What is the end of our doings?
Where are we trying to go?
Where do we put the emphasis and
where are our values focused?
For what end do we make sacrifices? Where is
my treasure and what do I love most in life?
What do I hate most in life and to what am I true?
Over and over the questions beat in
upon the waiting moment.
As we listen, floating up through all the jangling echoes
of our turbulence, there is a sound of another kind—
A deeper note which only the stillness
of the heart makes clear.
It moves directly to the core of our being.
Our questions are answered,
Our spirits refreshed, and we move back
into the traffic of our daily round
With the peace of the Eternal in our step.
How good it is to center down![28]

CLOSING PRAYER

Dear Lord, teach me how to slow down
and prayerfully reflect on you and your Word.
Speak to my heart as I ponder, muse,
and reflect on what you are doing in my life today.
Like Martha I have been distracted about many things,
but help me to be more like Mary to sit at your feet and hear
your word.
Help me to find you in the secret place of stillness and solitude.
Revive, renew, and restore my soul today in your name I pray.
Amen.

ESSENTIAL THOUGHT

Time alone with God, reflecting on the Scriptures, and the Daily Examen are three ways that we can cultivate prayerful reflection on the events of the day to detect God's presence and to discern his direction for us.

Practice

Before you go to sleep tonight, stop and spend some time alone with God in silent reflection. At first this might seem awkward, but allow yourself the time to prayerfully reflect on the events of the day. Then, begin to block out time each day for the next month to be alone with God for spiritual reflection.

Part Two

LEADERSHIP RHYTHMS

Chapter 4

LEADERSHIP ESSENTIALS FOR TODAY

"The way of the Christian leader is not the way of upward mobility in which our world has invested so much, but the way of downward mobility ending on the cross."
– HENRI NOUWEN

In many parts of the world, the church is in rapid decline, especially throughout most of the Western world. This crisis is widespread and has been going on for quite some time. It can be traced back to the rise of secularism and the collapse of Christendom in Western Europe—the shock waves of which are still being felt by church leaders. If the church is going to continue to have a future, it will need healthy leaders.

Based on our own person experience and study of leadership resilience, we want to offer you six marks we believe are essential for leaders to be able to navigate the present and future realities of the world in which we are living. This is not intended to be an exhaustive list; however, we do believe that it is important for leaders to understand these marks to be able to lead the church into the twenty-first century.

1. HOPEFUL LEADERSHIP

Many Christians have either resorted to a "gloom and doom" outlook or are simply pretending that nothing has changed.

We can find realistic hope that is rooted in Christ.

However, there is another way to look at the future: we need a realistic hope.[29] Megan Hyatt Miller reminds us, "Leaders require an accurate picture of the facts, but they also need to have confidence they can overcome even the worst news. That's realistic. And hopeful."[30] We do not have to be pessimistic or optimistic—we can find realistic hope that is rooted in Christ because he is the same, yesterday, today, and forever. Being hopeful doesn't mean that we stick our head in the sand and ignore the realities and challenges around us or that we give up on the world; rather, it means that we look in the face of our challenging circumstances with a realistic hope that comes from God.

In the movie *Rogue One: A Star Wars Story*, the leaders of the rebellion were facing overwhelming odds against them, and the main character, Jyn Erso, reminded them, "We have hope. Rebellions are built on hope." Similar to this, Christianity was built on hope. In the midst of war, persecution, or pandemic, hope is what has sustained the church throughout the ages. Romans 15:13 in *The Message* says, "May the God of green hope fill you up with joy, fill you up with peace, so that your believing lives, filled with the life-giving energy of the Holy Spirit, will brim over with hope!" Leaders of the future must have a realistic hope.

2. EMOTIONALLY HEALTHY LEADERSHIP

One of the greatest needs in the church today is for emotionally healthy leaders. Over the past decade, statistics have revealed that many Christian leaders are burned out. Some have committed moral failures. Others have simply walked away from the ministry.[31] I (Winfield) have been researching and teaching on leadership burnout for a decade, which is one of the main reasons we have written this book. We don't just want to help leaders survive but also to help them thrive in the new normal.

One of the primary reasons for burnout is that too many leaders are emotionally unhealthy. In his book *The Emotionally Healthy Leader*, Peter Scazzero says, "The emotionally unhealthy leader is someone who operates in a continuous state of emotional and spiritual deficit, lacking emotional maturity and a 'being *with* God' sufficient to sustain their 'doing *for* God.'"[32] In contrast, an emotionally healthy leader is one who leads "from a deep and transformed inner life."[33] Healthy leadership involves attending to our inner life and knowing ourselves as well as knowing God.

Sadly, too many Christian leaders around the world lack emotional health. According to Scazzero, emotional health is concerned with the following:

- Naming, recognizing, and managing our own feelings;
- Identifying with and having active compassion for others;
- Initiating and maintaining close and meaningful relationships;
- Breaking free from self-destructive patterns;
- Being aware of how our past impacts our present;

- Developing the capacity to express our thoughts and feelings clearly;
- Respecting and loving others without having to change them;
- Asking for what we need, want, or prefer clearly, directly, and respectfully;
- Accurately self-assessing our strengths, limits, and weaknesses and freely sharing them with others;
- Learning the capacity to resolve conflict maturely and negotiate solutions that consider the perspectives of others;
- Distinguishing and appropriately expressing our spirituality with our sexuality and sensuality;
- Grieving well.[34]

The key task of an emotionally healthy Christian is the "knowledge of God and of ourselves."[35] Knowing ourselves is

Emotional intelligence probes the depths of identity

sometimes referred to as emotional intelligence. This does not pertain to our cognitive intelligence but is another kind of "smart": our *emotional* intelligence. This emotional intelligence reflects the capability of individuals to recognize and use their own emotional information to manage and adapt to various environments in order to achieve success. Rather than focusing on your ability to perform tasks, emotional intelligence probes the depths of identity to ensure that at your very core, you possess the character, stamina, and adaptability to succeed as a leader.

In the words of Drs. Travis Bradberry and Jean Greaves, "Emotional intelligence is your ability to recognize and understand emotions in yourself and others, and your ability to use this awareness to manage your behavior and relationships."[36]

They believe that emotional intelligence affects how we govern our behavior, navigate social complexities, and make personal decisions that achieve positive results. According to Bradberry and Greaves, emotional intelligence is comprised of four core skills that pair up under two primary competencies: personal competence and social competence.

Another important key to emotional health is what Edwin Friedman, in his book *A Failure of Nerve*, called "differentiation." Differentiation is an important skill for leaders because it involves the ability to remain connected to people, yet not have your reaction or behaviors determined by them. Friedman says, "a well-differentiated leader is less likely to become lost in the anxious emotional processes swirling about. I mean someone who can be separate while still remaining connected and, therefore, can maintain a modifying, non-anxious, and sometimes challenging presence."[37] Emotionally healthy leaders have the ability to calmly differentiate themselves from the demands and voices around them. In the challenging times we are living in, what could be more needed in a leader today?

3. CONTEMPLATIVE LEADERSHIP

Leaders are too often people of action, but rarely men and women of contemplation and prayer.

Contemplative prayer is important for leaders because even doing a good work for the Lord can be a distraction if we do not allow time to rest. After the disciples returned from a busy missionary journey, Jesus told them to "Come with me by yourselves to a quiet place and get some rest" (Mark 6:31). They had been busy, and Jesus knew that they needed rest for their weary souls. Spiritual burnout occurs when we do not give ourselves time to rest from our daily routine.

Contemplative prayer should flow into contemplative action. One of the greatest modern examples of contemplative leadership is Dr. Martin Luther King, Jr. At the age of thirty-five, King became the youngest man to receive the Nobel Peace Prize for his leadership in the American Civil Rights movement. His prophetic words inspired a generation and resulted in legal and social change that empowered Black Americans who had been disenfranchised and persecuted for centuries. One evening when he was ready to give up, he had a deep encounter with God that changed his life. He recounts this experience in a sermon entitled "Our God Is Able," where he tells a very personal story that gave him the strength and courage to continue on with his fight for justice and equality:

> The words I spoke to God that midnight are still vivid in my memory. "I am here taking a stand for what I believe is right. But now I am afraid. The people are looking to me for leadership, and if I stand before them without strength, they too will falter. I am at the end of my powers. I have nothing left. I have come to the point where I can't face it alone." At that moment I experienced the presence of the Divine as I had never experienced him. It seemed as though I could hear the quiet assurance of an inner voice, saying, "Stand up for righteousness, stand up for truth. God will be at your side forever." Almost at once my fears passed from me. My uncertainty disappeared. I was ready to face anything. The outer situation remained the same, but God had given me inner calm.[38]

This is a beautiful example of contemplative action.
There are many examples of contemplative action throughout
history where leaders led out of a place of deep contemplative
spirituality.

4. ADAPTIVE LEADERSHIP

The Bible reminds us how unwelcome disruptions come to the
Church and although we fight against it and hope that God
would never let terrible things happen—disruptive change
results in a deepening and expanding of spiritual and numerical
growth for the Church. As the nation of Israel was heading into
the uncharted territory of the Promised Land, God encouraged
Joshua four times to "be strong and courageous" (Josh.1:6, 7,
9, 18). Just like Joshua, we live in uncertain times, where many
people are struggling to navigate the challenges of the new
realities in which we live. We are in uncharted territory and
have never "been this way before" either. We need courageous
leaders who will take us into the future!

So what is a courageous leader? According to Professor
Nancy Koehn, "A courageous leader is an individual who's
capable of making themselves better and stronger when the
stakes are high and circumstances turn against that person.
Courageous leaders are not cowed or intimidated. They realize
that, in the midst of turbulence, there lies an extraordinary
opportunity to grow and rise."[39] Based on her research, Brené
Brown defines courageous and daring leadership as, "the
courage to show up when you can't predict the future."[40]
Today's world requires courageous leaders who are willing to
lead when they can't foresee the outcome.

In our world, it is so important to be flexible and adaptable to the needs of others. Leaders of the future must be able to adapt to rapidly changing environment. Ron Heifetz and Marty Linsky define adaptive leadership as the ability of "individuals and organizations to adapt and thrive in challenging environments."[41] The concept of *adaptivity* is an organic concept drawn from biology in which living things adapt to survive.

The Old and New Testaments are also based on an organic worldview. The church is the spiritual and living Body of

> The church is the spiritual and living Body of Christ.

Christ. Like all healthy organisms, it requires numerous systems and structures that work together to fulfill its intended purpose and overall health. Just as the physical body has to have an organic structure to hold it together while allowing it to grow and develop, so the body of Christ must have an organic structure that can do the same.

Leaders need to be flexible and adaptive to the changes that are swirling around us. Leonard Sweet says, "We must develop ministries that continually adjust and change with our continually changing culture."[42] In a similar way, leaders need to be both courageous and able to adapt to the ongoing changes and challenges around us. If not, our growth is at stake.

5. CULTURALLY SENSITIVITY LEADERSHIP

We live in an increasingly diverse world where leaders will need cultural sensitivity to navigate various levels of social complexity. With the rise of globalization, the world has become increasingly multiethnic and diverse. For instance, with more than 337 languages represented in country, the United States has become the most multicultural and multilingual nation on earth.[43] In many urban contexts, missional leaders will have to cross racial, cultural, and socioeconomic lines to reach their communities. Multiethnic ministry points to the beautiful picture promised in the book of Revelation where people from every nation, tribe, and language praise God in unison with one another. This portrait is essential to the Christian faith. No matter what kind of church we attend or are thinking about planting, we should all find ways to reach across ethnic, racial, cultural, and economic barriers.

According to Gary Collins:

> Culture might be viewed as a collection of the beliefs, customs, values, and ways of thinking that are common within a group of people. A more formal definition describes culture as a common history, physical environment, and place of living, language, and religion that shapes members of a society so that they develop and share common assumptions, values, beliefs, and worldviews.[44]

From issues relating to race, gender, and politics, there is a growing need for leaders to develop their "cultural intelligence"—which refers to a person's capacities to understand and effectively respond to the beliefs, values, attitudes, and behaviors of others who differ from them.[45]

To be an effective leader in today's world, you will need to be able to learn the skills and develop the ability to understand and appreciate diverse cultures and contexts and be able to work across national, ethnic, and political lines. This will become increasingly essential in our global world. Every context is different, so it is crucial to be able to understand and engage the unique culture and context in the location where you live and work. This begins from the leaders' own self-awareness, their listening to others, and their seeking to understand

and appreciate the cultural perspective of those they seek to influence.

6. SERVANT LEADERSHIP

Finally, leaders of the future need to be servants.[46] Unfortunately, our individualistic society has caused us to neglect the need to put others above ourselves. For our culture, serving is revolutionary because it goes against the natural tendency toward self-preservation and elevation. The mind of a servant constantly looks around and asks, "What can I do for others?" instead of, "What can they do for me?" We find this mindset pervading the life of Jesus. He set the ultimate example by living out this verse: "The Son of Man did not come to be served, but to serve, and to give his life as a ransom for many" (Mark 10:45). Christian leaders must strive to be like Jesus, our perfect example. By engaging in faithful servanthood, we, as the Body of Christ, become Christ's representatives to a lost world.

As a whole, the Church should be an army of servants who are making a positive difference in their families, community, and world. With a commitment to servant leadership, we are bound to witness a revolution that will transform our communities and demonstrate the love of Christ for the world to see. Henri Nouwen reminds us that "a whole new type of leadership is asked for in the church of tomorrow, a leadership that is not modelled on the power games of the world, but on the servant-leader Jesus, who came to give his life for the salvation of many."[47] Nothing could be more critical for missional leadership of today than that. In the next chapter, we are going to introduce you to an effective approach for solving difficult problems and cultivating a missional imagination.

CLOSING PRAYER

Dear Lord, I pray that you would use me as a vessel of honor.
I am willing to be used for you in any of that you want.
Give me the gifts that I need to accomplish your will.
Demonstrate your glory through me today.
Thank you that you still give gifts to men and women who seek your face.
Touch me Holy Ghost and let me live and act in your name.
In the name of the Father, the Son, and the Holy Spirit. Amen.

ESSENTIAL THOUGHT

Being a healthy missional leader will help you be able to navigate the present-future realities of the world in which we are living.

Practice

Being a healthy leader is about developing healthy behaviors and practices in your life. Here are a few practices that will help you grow as a healthy leader:

1. Rather than being cynical, focus on having a realistic hope.
2. Ask a few close friends how they would describe your emotional intelligence.
3. Face one area of your life you know you need to change.

4. Intentionally have a conversation with people who are different from you.
5. Try to be kind, generous, and empathetic each day, and look for opportunities to suspend your own needs and wants for the sake of others.

Chapter 5

MISSIONAL DESIGN THINKING

"We cannot solve our problems with the same thinking we used when we created them."
— ALBERT EINSTEIN

During the past two thousand years, the Church has grown from a few hundred believers to over a billion believers. An important part of this growth was the essential practice of the Church developing its missional creativity. Doing so helped Christians rediscover what it means for mission to take on an incarnational presence in a particular time and place. As Jesus showed with the analogy of the new cloth in Mark 2:21— that the new religion of Christianity cannot coexist with the old customs and practices of Judaism—the new entity of the twenty-first century church must create its own forms and practices. This "new cloth" of Christianity is not to be used to patch up existing practices, but rather create a new garment for the needs of the day. These new garments must have the commands of Jesus as their theological backbone and be guided by the Holy Spirit.

History informs us that restructuring the local church by the pouring out of love through new wineskins must be unpinned by a renewal in the Holy Spirit. For it is life in the

Holy Spirit that guides the Church boldly into risk and adventure. This corporate life in the Holy Spirit ensures leaders depend on the fullness of joy

missional creativity flows directly from the work of the Holy Spirit

(Ps. 16:8–9, 11) experienced as a place of nearness (closeness) and dearness (affection) to God through Jesus. Cultivating missional creativity flows directly from the work of the Holy Spirit in our lives and from our relationship with Jesus Christ.

To engage in missional creativity, we need a biblically-grounded, grace-filled, contextually-sensitive, re-reading of the Bible to understand and participate in God's mission, in this new century and in a hurting world that is dearly loved by God. Today, there is resurgence of God's people's approach to the idea of developing new Christian communities with an open heart, an open mind, and an open will as they cross the valley of transformation together. By harvesting thought-streams from Scripture, theology, and missional history, and looking to other disciplines for ideas, church leaders are weaving new church concepts that are complementing existing forms of church. As previous chapters have highlighted the roots of missional spirituality, in this chapter we will explore the importance of missional *imagination*, and we'll focus on what we call "Missional Design Thinking."

HISTORY OF DESIGN THINKING

We want to introduce you to an innovative way of solving problems and leading change called design thinking, which is a tool that we have used over the past fifteen years to help thousands of missional leaders across three continents. The concept emerged from an exploration analysis of theory and practice in a range of disciplines and sciences as a means of addressing the human, the technological, and the strategic innovation needs of our time. Complex problems require a collaborative method that involve gaining a deep understanding of humans, and design thinking is a time-tested method for solving difficult problems and finding solutions.[48]

In 1991, design and consulting firm Innovation Design Engineering Organization (IDEO) was formed. Emerging from the work at Stanford Design School, IDEO is now widely accepted as the organization that brought design thinking into the mainstream. In 1992, the Head of the School of Design at Carnegie Mellon University, Richard Buchanan, published his article, *Wicked Problems in Design Thinking*, which discussed the origins of design thinking, how the science developed over time from the Renaissance period, and how collaboration between various disciplines can be jointly applied to new problems.[49]

At present, design thinking is gaining ground rapidly. Universities, business schools, and forward-thinking companies have adopted the methodology to varying degrees. It is fair to say that the Church at large, as well as theological colleges, have been slow to adopt this methodology. Over the last few years, we have seen how this approach can help leaders reflect on how the local church might better serve its neighborhood by observing the needs, wants, desires, pains, and gains of those they seek to love. We believe within the next five years, design thinking methods will be firmly ensconced in the practices of those churches that thrive in our new missional age that requires one developing a healthy missional creativity. In Scripture and in church history, we see examples similar to design thinking about how it can yield some of the richest opportunities for missional imagination.

THE MISSIONAL DESIGN THINKING PROCESS

Missional Design Thinking starts with a problem or a challenge. Problems are identified through closely listening to people and inviting them to share their struggles. The next step is the "deep dive": intensive learning by observing people involved in the problem. From a design-thinking perspective, it is not enough to ask people about their behavior, as people often don't recognize their own assumptions and patterns; one must watch how they live and what they do. Out of what is noticed in observation, collaborative teams engage in a process of rapid prototyping.

These are makeshift solutions that take concrete physical form, not just beautiful concepts sketched on paper. Missional Design thinking recognizes something very important: people learn through tangible experiences, not just ideas. The rapid prototypes are small experiments whose sole purpose is learning. Missional Design thinkers realize that seeing, holding, tasting, and trying out things sparks the best insights. Failure is expected in these experiments, as nothing is finished yet.

We know that collaboration in the Church is rarely easy. Yet, we passionately believe a design-thinking approach to solving problems holds some key lessons for the Church. Often times, churches (and their leaders) act independently efficiently rather than collaboratively. Missional Design thinking can help the Church tackle complex problems by bringing together diverse perspectives and skill sets.

Missional Design thinking is about joining up with people where they are in the world, attending carefully to their ordinary lives, and improvising solutions to challenges they face. Once this "way of being" is embraced by the Church, leadership teams get used to finding new ways to collaborate with the Holy Spirit in their neighborhood. We tend to believe the myth that only some people are creative and innovative (and this myth will always suit those who seek to hold power over others); however, innovation and the Church have always been present throughout our history. Integrating a culture of missional imagination in your context is not so much a matter of a solitary genius receiving a bolt of inspiration as it is ordinary people joining up with other ordinary people and attending to the realities of daily life.

APPLYING MISSIONAL DESIGN THINKING

Culturally we are in the early stages of change for the church in this new digital age. Naivety and self-interest are holding back the missional imagination of many Christian leaders. Naivety and reluctance to adapt is not unexpected in times of change; remember what Henry Ford said? "If I asked people what they wanted, they would have said a faster horse".

If we are good missionaries, we have to get as close to people as possible. We need to be Christian leaders who participate and attend to our neighborhoods' daily and fast-changing needs. Missional Design thinkers are empathic and support processes of a "people first" approach, thinking beyond the scope of purely rational pathways to create solutions that make a noticeable difference in existing situations.

Furthermore, the Missional Design thinker understands they must radically disrupt instead of just making small tweaks to the current process. Rather than the "same old, same old" mentality, a paradigm shift is needed both within their hearts and the hearts of their fellow Christians to make a noticeable difference in their society.

Here are a few guiding principles for applying Missional Design Thinking:

- In the Bible, we read that God is on a mission to redeem our world. Hence, we are invited and charged with being part of a community of believers created by the Spirit that is missional and sent to participate in God's mission in the world. As we enter this new digital age, a design thinking methodology enables leaders to create environments that support the vulnerability and experiential Spirit necessary to develop creative solutions to being God's people in a particular time and place.
- Empathy and incarnation are the heart of Missional Design Thinking – because it starts with a deep dive into the wants, needs, pains and gains of those we seek to love and serve.
- Missional Design Thinking releases us from 'it has always been done this way' by creating cycles of deep listening, testing new ideas, and reflecting on learnings.
- The process requires everyone to adopt a beginners mindset; the best Missional Design processes have the most diverse voices.
- Missional Design Thinking creates a culture of allowing and indeed expecting failure—the simple act of letting each other the grace to fail opens up a myriad of new solutions.

- Evaluation becomes open and curious, rather than closed and fearful.
- Missional Design Thinking, by its very nature, is uncomplicated and straightforward. The starting point is two or more disciples being motivated to reflect on God's mission through scripture, prayer, and everyday relationships.

We have successfully utilized design thinking techniques in the church to inspire leaders' missional creativity as they created innovative new communities of faith. Here is an overview of the five stages process that we have adapted to our Missional Design Thinking model. It can be used or adapted for any organization, whether it be your personal life, a church, or a business, to build your team's confidence to tackle complex challenges.

MISSIONAL DESIGN THINKING: A FIVE STAGE PROCESS

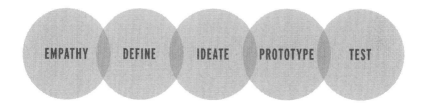

1. Empathize. Begin with empathy, which simply means showing that you care. It is essential to have empathy for those you are trying to serve, and for the problem you're trying to solve. From a Missional Design Thinking perspective, it is not enough to ask people about their behavior, as people often don't recognize their own assumptions and patterns. One must watch how they live and what they do. Empathy is crucial to a design process because it reminds us that we are attempting to find real solutions to real people's real problems. This helps us set aside our own assumptions and biases to gain real insight into others' needs.

2. Define. You have to begin with the problem if you want to find the solution. Problems are at the very heart of Missional Design Thinking because complex problems require collaborative methods that involve gaining a deep understanding of people. While it is tempting to go for quick and easy consensus, true transformation requires moving beyond familiar solutions by welcoming diversity and embracing more unfamiliar options. The process for problem-solving is using one's creativity. Ask yourself, "What is the problem I want to solve? Inspire your team to think about who you're designing a solution for and what they actually need. This is also referred to as "the problem." You have to begin with the problem if you want to find the solution.

3. Ideate. Now that you have identified the problem, you are ready to begin generating ideas. This process is commonly referred to as "ideation." In this stage you begin asking, "How might we . . . ?" Ideation is where creativity and imagination come in. In the ideation stage, we may generate many ideas and consider many different options, so the key is to be bold and be prepared to give up on what once seemed to be a good idea. Think outside the box and look for alternative ways to view the problem, and identify innovative solutions to the problem statement you've created.

4. Prototype. Out of what is noticed in observation, collaborative teams engage in rapid prototyping. The rapid prototypes are small experiments whose sole purpose is learning. Prototyping helps us learn, solve disagreements, and test hypotheses quickly and with minimal repercussions. The aim of the prototype phase is to try to identify the best possible solution for each problem. During this phase, you and your team should try to produce scaled-down prototype to investigate the ideas you've generated so you can determine what works and what doesn't. Missional Design Thinkers realize that seeing, holding, tasting, and trying out things sparks the best insights. Failure is fully expected in these experiments, as nothing is finished yet. These are makeshift solutions that take concrete physical form, not just beautiful concepts sketched on paper. Indeed, prototypes are tried out with the knowledge that the approach might not work.

5. *Test.* The final phase is implementation where you test the prototype in real life and with real people. In this phase, we aim to learn how to make our prototype better – we seek to fail quickly and cheaply! In traditional learning forms, the result is concrete and final. However, in design thinking, the testing phase is where you find out what works and what does not work. You may test out many versions, learn from the people you seek to impact, refine prototypes based on those learnings, and test again. It's an iterative process. By implementing prototypes that seem to work in our cultural context, we can then roll out a new way of living.

CONCLUSION

There is a belief out there that leaders who manage change well are always optimistic and confident. Yet that hasn't been my (Mark's) experience at all. Creativity and innovation aren't all about fun and being certain of what you're doing. Instead, it is about creating environments and processes that support the vulnerability and experiential Spirit necessary to develop creative solutions to being God's people in a particular time and place.

Managing change takes a lot of effort to create new mental models, and integrating a culture of innovation and creativity into church culture is a tough task even for the most creative leaders. Being in that state of disequilibrium is hard work. Though, somehow, just knowing that you're in that state of disequilibrium makes it feel less stressful. When the signs of frustration and impatience come bubbling up, know that a new state of knowledge and prompting of the Holy Spirit can be on the other side of uncertainty.

A creative mindset can be a powerful force for the Church to look beyond the status quo.

A creative mindset can be a powerful force for the Church to look beyond the status quo. We have repeatedly observed Christians using creativity to fuel their missional imagination and paint a picture of a Jesus-inspired future that cherishes the past, adorns the present, and constructs the future.

We hope this chapter has given you a glimpse into how Christian leaders can adopt a posture of missional imagination through the lens of Missional Design Thinking.

CLOSING PRAYER

Dear Lord, so draw our hearts to you, so guide our minds,
so fill our imaginations, so control our wills,
that we may be wholly yours, utterly dedicated unto you;
and then use us, we pray you, as you will,
and always to your glory and the welfare of your people;
through our Lord and Savior Jesus Christ. Amen.

ESSENTIAL THOUGHT

Missional imagination helps us find new ways of being the Church in uncertain times with the knowledge that we serve a creative God.

Practice

What is the biggest problem are you facing in life or ministry that you need to solve today? Get out a sheet of paper or a journal and take some time to stop and apply the five-step design-thinking process outlined in this chapter.

Part Three

CORPORATE RHYTHMS

Chapter 6

GUIDING OTHERS IN THE WAY

"I want a guide who listens to God as well as to me, who is attuned to the promptings of the Spirit when we meet."
– MARJORIE J. THOMPSON

Take a moment to think about a person who made a difference in your life. Was it a teacher, a neighbor, a soccer coach, a pastor, or someone else? What did they do to make a difference? I (Winfield) could tell you about some examples of people making a *negative difference*, but I could also tell you about many good examples, like my high school art teacher, Rosa Kennedy. I was a troubled teenager who almost dropped out of school. I needed guidance and a mentor. Rosa saw my potential as a human being and took me under her wing, teaching me how to paint. Art became a means of grace that pointed me back toward God. I would not be who I am today had she not taken the time to teach me the value of art and am forever thankful for her influence on my life.

More than ever before we need spiritual guides who can point us to the life-giving way of Christ.

In a chaotic, post-COVID-19 world, Christian leaders need to see themselves

> *We need spiritual guides who can point us to the life-giving way of Christ.*

as spiritual guides. There is an ancient Christian practice in which a spiritually mature person (often called a spiritual director) assists the person seeking spiritual direction in their process of spiritual growth by listening and asking thought-provoking questions.[50]

We see examples of spiritual guidance throughout the Bible, whether it be Elijah and Elisha, Moses and Jethro, Paul, Lydia, Barnabas, and Timothy (to name just a few). In particular, we see this in the life of Jesus: Jesus provides spiritual guidance for his disciples through conversations that employed thought provoking questions. For example, Matthew records sixty-five questions; Mark records forty-five questions; Luke records seventy-three questions; and John records forty-five questions. From this we see that questions were at the heart of Jesus' discipleship methodology. Jesus' questions were designed to lead his disciples toward inner transformation and deeper into God's mission.

Jesus was intimately involved in the lives of his disciples as they followed him. His training method was spending time with his disciples in order to build deep relationships with them. Jesus had no formal training or education. Jesus guided his disciples and whenever they returned from a ministry trip, they would report to him what they had done (see Mark 6:30). This allowed a time for the disciples to reflect, review, and receive instruction from Jesus. In the same ways coaching is still an important part of leadership development for missional leaders today.

Some of the earliest mentions of spiritual direction come from the fourth century, where John Cassian provided some of the earliest recorded guidelines on the Christian practice of spiritual direction. The Eastern Orthodoxy tradition still honors the role of a "spiritual director" or "elder." In the fifth century in Ireland, early Celtic saints such as Patrick, Brigid, Columba of Iona and Cuthbert of Lindisfarne emphasized the role of the *anam cara*, or soul friend, as central in Celtic spiritual life.

The role of spiritual direction is to uncover what God is doing in a person's life. Author Margaret Gunther says, "When in doubt, I always assume that God is at work, that is, the person is pregnant."[51] This means that God is always at work in our lives, even if we don't see or feel it. A spiritual director helps us discern where God is at work. Spiritual direction isn't concerned with pie-in-the-sky spirituality, but seeks to bring the spiritual into everyday life. According to author Alan Jacobs, "The art of spiritual direction lies in our uncovering the obvious in everyday lives and in realizing that everyday events are the means by which God tries to reach us."[52] Today, spiritual direction is a rich Christian tradition still being used and adapted in many places around the world.[53] This tradition is still alive through leaders who are committed to pouring their life into others.

GUIDING OTHERS THROUGH COACHING

In this chapter we want to unpack the coaching relationship. One of the biggest challenges for contemporary leaders is the loneliness that can come from leadership. Healthy leaders know that they can't go it alone. Every missional leader needs a coach, a mentor, or a spiritual director. This is why coaching is so important. Leadership is hard; don't do it alone. I (Winfield) tell leaders all the time that everyone needs a Paul (a seasoned coach) and a Timothy (a younger leader that they are coaching). Why, you may ask? The reason is simple: to continue growing as a leader, we need someone coaching us and we need to be coaching someone else to help others grow.

In the following pages, we want to share with you an approach that we have adapted for guiding others that brings together lessons from spiritual direction with leadership coaching practices. Based on more than four decades of working with leaders from around the world, we have developed a unique model called "Missional Formation Coaching," which is a reflective approach to coaching designed to help leaders thrive by promoting healthy rhythms that connect spiritual and missional practices. In this chapter, we explore how you can help become a spiritual guide by offering four core competencies: praying, listening, questioning, and reflecting. Let's explore these competencies, which are foundational to the work of being a spiritual guide for others, as we bring together the best of spiritual direction and leadership coaching.

We like to speak of coaching as a relationship. Coaching in its most basic essence is a formal relationship for leaders. The problem is that some people think coaching is simply one more task, like checking an item off a "to do" list. But that isn't really coaching at all. We should think of coaching in intimate terms, like a conversation between close friends. What are some words that you think of when you think of an intimate friendship? You will probably think of words like loving, caring, sincere, and personal. Coaching should not be dry or stuffy; it should be warm and intimate.

Think of coaching as a relationship, rather than a business transaction. It involves a relationship built on trust and mutual respect.

Coaching is a relationship that helps leaders develop their God-given potential so that they grow individually and make a valuable contribution to the kingdom of God. It is an alliance that is designed by the person being coached and the coach for the purpose of helping the coachee realize their full kingdom potential. Coaching identifies the current learning agendas between where you are and where you discern your future story is calling you. Coaching is, at its best, a very collaborative journey between the coach and the person being coached—a journey focused on helping individuals achieve their goals for their life, their family, and their mission.

Missional Formation Coaching is not a one-size-fits-all approach to coaching. It can be used in any number of ways, including informal, formal, and group coaching relationships. Each of these three approaches are important, but serve similar—yet different—functions. The important thing to take into consideration when trying to discern which type of coaching to use is the answer to the question, "What fits best the context of the person(s) being coached?"

The most personalized form of coaching is a one-to-one coaching relationship between the coach and the person being coached. One-to-one coaching is basically the process of coming alongside a person to help them discover God's purpose for their life and ministry, then continuing to cooperate with them to help that become a reality. One-to-one coaching can be either informal or formal.

An *informal* coaching relationship is a more organic approach to coaching and involves a less formal mode of engagement, such as the relationship between a pastor and a church member or between a missional leader and someone they are discipling. This approach to coaching usually does not involve a contract or any type of payment, but rather a simple agreement between the coach and the coachee. Informal coaching is more similar to spiritual direction and disciple making than it is to secular coaching.

A *formal* coaching relationship is one that involves a higher level of professionalism and requires more experience and training on the part of the coach. Someone offering professional coaching should strongly consider pursuing coach training or certification to help ensure that they are properly trained and equipped for the task of being an effective coach (see the "Conclusion: Next Steps" section of this book). Due to the professional nature of the formal coaching relationship, it also requires a structured agreement between the coach and coachee to help establish the expectations and boundaries of the coaching relationship. Depending on the coach, formal coaching often involves payment for coaching services.

Group coaching brings the coaching conversation into a small group context of three to six people. We call this "coaching in community." Disciples are made in community, not isolation. Perhaps the reason why many leaders struggle with making disciples is that they themselves do not know how to live in community. God made us to live in community with others. Group coaching is great way to receive coaching in a dynamic, small group environment with other leaders, and it gives those who are a part of the coaching community access to different viewpoints and approaches to problems and challenges.

Another form of group coaching is often called a learning community, which is a little bit larger in size. Learning communities are about connecting, learning, and growing in a community with other leaders. Facilitated by a master coach, learning communities are one of the most effective ways to grow as a leader because they enable participants to engage in peer-to-peer learning and network with other missional leaders (ideally ten to fifteen people). Learning communities are usually comprised of leaders with similar roles or interests and last six to twelve months.

Informal, formal, and group coaching are all valid and important types of coaching, each providing a unique service to the coach. Both of us have had numerous informal, formal, and group coaching relationships throughout our lives and have helped coach others in both informal and formal capacities. It all depends on the context and needs of the people being coached. For instance, a pastor can bring leaders from their congregation together to form a learning community, while a professional coach may decide to only coach one person at a time. Therefore, we advocate the need for each of these types of coaching.

FOUR COACHING COMPETENCIES

1. Begin and End with Prayer. Coaching begins and ends with prayer. Many people spend only a few minutes each day reading and meditating on the Bible; often, this is not enough. Sitting and prayerfully meditating on God's Word puts the cares of this world in proper perspective and opens us up to allowing God to speak to us. In his book *In the Name of Jesus,* Henri Nouwen says, "If there is any focus that the Christian leader of the future will need, it is the discipline of dwelling in the presence of the One who keeps saying, 'Do you love me?' This is the discipline of contemplative prayer."[54]

Prayer is essential to the coaching relationship because without prayer, we cannot listen to God or others. Real prayer is listening. Prayer helps distinguish Christian coaching from secular coaching because it brings God into the coaching process. The coach should prayerfully prepare themselves before each session, then begin each session with prayer, inviting God's Spirit to come and guide the coaching session. In prayer, we open ourselves up to the work of the Holy Spirit and allow him to speak to us. Thomas Merton rightly reminds us that the first duty of an effective director "is to see to his own interior life and take time for prayer and meditation, since he will never be able to give to others what he does not possess himself."[55]

Prayer can and should precede the coaching situation. The coach and person being coached should be prepared already by maintaining a lifestyle of prayer. However, there are times when emergency situations occur and we find ourselves in a place where we are unable to take time out to pray in advance. In a situation like this, it is helpful to pray there and then with the person you are coaching. You might be in a car, a hospital room, or perhaps in the grocery store. Prayer should always be primary to any coaching situation.

Prayer saturates both the coach and the person being coached with the presence of God. It invites the living God to come in and take control of the situation. Prayer brings God into the crisis. Oftentimes, even if we don't know what to do or haven't the words to say, the sweet presence of the Lord is enough. I (Winfield) have known times where words were not enough, but all that was needed was God's comforting presence. Therefore, it is the task of the coach not only to use words to heal but to provide the means by which the Lord can come and be known. Prayer should precede, be a part of, and follow the coaching conversation. It is not enough to just pray at the beginning; there needs to be an openness toward being led by the Spirit throughout the counseling session.

> *Prayer saturates both the coach and the person being coached with the presence of God.*

2. Listen Deeply. Deep listening is essential for both those being coached and for those who are coaching. There are two types of listening: one with the human ear and one with a spiritual ear. Over time, we have become accustomed to listening with our outward ear at the expense of our interior ear. The result is that we have lost the art of spiritual listening, and we need to recover it. Spiritual listening involves two interconnected parts: praying and listening.

Deep listening flows out of prayer. This is sometimes referred to as "double listening," which involves listening to God and listening to culture. God often speaks through events and circumstances, and we need to have the space to reflect on what is being said. For instance, what is God saying to the church about racism? What is God saying to the church about the COVID-19 pandemic? How are we to respond to these real issues out of love and compassion, rather than out of a place of outrage and division? These are the questions of our age. According to John Stott,

> Double listening is the faculty of listening to two voices at the same time, the voice of God through Scripture and the voices of men and women around us. These voices will often contradict one another, but our purpose in listening to them both is to discover how they relate to each other. Double listening is indispensable to Christian discipleship and Christian mission.[56]

Double listening will help us know how to respond in a redemptive way, rather than just reacting to circumstances or going along with the world. Contemplative action will help leaders of the future respond to the burning needs of the day out of a place of prayer, rather than anxiety.

At the core of coaching is the person and work of the Holy Spirit. Jesus said, "When he, the Spirit of truth, comes, he will guide you into all truth" (John 16:13). The Holy Spirit wants to give us wisdom, guidance, and direction in the coaching session. Many times, what a person is saying may not be what they are really mean, or they may be hiding behind their words. Therefore, it is essential to invite the presence and leading of the Holy Spirit to come and guide you in the coaching session.

The Spirit is a guide who leads us in the way we should live our lives. We are confident that it is God's deepest desire that we seek his wisdom and will in every area of our lives. Take time out of each day to ask the Holy Spirit to guide you. Begin by praying each morning, "Holy Spirit, lead and guide me today." He will guide you if you will ask and be open to his leading. Listen for God's voice to speak into your life. God usually doesn't speak in an audible voice from heaven. He speaks with a quiet voice. It can be as faint as a whisper, and if we are not careful, we will miss it.

Here is an acronym that will help you become a better active listener:

LISTEN

L   *Let go of distractions*
I   *Cultivate Intimacy with God*
S   *Be open to the Spirit*
T   *Build Time and Trust*
E   *Always Encourage*
N   *Discern Next steps*

3. Ask Questions. Equally important to listening is asking questions. Margaret Guenther, whom we mentioned above, eloquently reminds us, "Simple, direct questions that cut to the heart of the matter are part of the spiritual tradition."[57] Questions are an important part of life, and you are never too old or too young to ask them. When we grow up, we typically have a lot more questions than answers. That's why children ask so many questions—like, "How can birds fly?" or "Where do people go when they die?" or "Why does the sun set and rise?" or "Where is heaven?" Good questions provoke us to think deeply about God, ourselves, and others.

Again, we can turn to the ministry of Jesus Christ for the art of asking questions. In the Gospels, we are reminded that Jesus often used simple questions to teach profound truths. Questions were at the heart of Jesus' discipleship methodology. He didn't provide all the answers. Instead, like all good coaches, Jesus used powerful, thought-provoking questions to teach valuable truths to his disciples.

> *Jesus often used simple questions to teach profound truths.*

Questions are natural ways to find out the basic answers to life. Questions are also an essential part of growing in your faith. They help us discover the mysteries of our faith. They are how we learn, grow, and ultimately come to believe. Once you stop asking questions, you stop learning, growing, and believing. Rather than providing only answers, a good coach knows how to ask the right questions that will help the person being coached discover the right answers for themselves. More importantly, the right questions help us reflect more clearly on what God is doing in our lives and in our ministry. Effective missional coaches ask questions that reveal the information needed for the most benefit to the coaching relationship.

4. Reflecting. Finally, coaching is not just spiritual or pragmatic but is also rooted in theological reflection that can assist leaders to understand the distinctive social, cultural, spiritual, and contextual factors of respondents and the meaning behind the practices of the church and the world. John Swinton and Harriet Mowat define practical theology as "critical, theological reflection on the practices of the church as they interact with the world, with a view to ensuring and enabling faithful participation in God's redemptive practices in, to and for the world."[58]

Practical theology brings together theory and practice in a deep, theologically-reflective way. It recognizes that practice cannot be divorced from theory because "human experience is a 'place' where the gospel is grounded, embodied, interpreted and lived out."[59] Practical theology refuses to bifurcate theology and practice, instead seeks to bring theology to bear on the human experience and practices of the church.

Craig Dykstra and Dorothy C. Bass define Christian practices as "things Christian people do together over time to address fundamental human needs in response to and in the light of God's active presence for the life of the world."[60] This definition emphasizes that Christian practices are meant to be communal and social in nature, as well as reminding us that they are theologically grounded in God and the world. Understanding the complex situations where real people live, interact, and practice their faith is essential to the task of practical theology and therefore also to Missional Formation Coaching.

In *Introducing Practical Theology: Mission, Ministry, and the Life of the Church*, Pete Ward reminds us that practical theology is fundamentally ecclesial and theological in nature.[61]

Ward also believes that the field of practical theology should also start with everyday life and be expanded to include the canon of practical theology by inviting participation from those outside its academic guild.[62] This is one of Ward's greatest contributions, the reminder that practical theology "arises from and seeks to inform the pastoral practice of the church."[63]

For Ward and others, everyday practical theology is "deeply embedded in the practice of faith."[64] Ward concludes by highlighting the outcome of practical theology, namely "the transformation of individuals and communities," which is expressed in various forms that include "living, action, prayer, songs, and preaching."[65] Ward's unique approach to practical theology ensures that practical theology remains practical, lived, and rooted in everyday life as opposed to merely theoretical. Practical theology offers a framework that is deeply beneficial to those who are offering coaching to others by asking deep theological questions.

FOUR QUESTIONS

Here are four core questions that we have found very helpful to reflect on the practices of ministry.

1. "What is going on?"
2. "Why is this going on?"
3. "What ought to be going on?"
4. "How might we respond?"

Each of these four questions is the focus of the four following theological tasks of practical theological interpretation.[66] These questions offer a fourfold model that will provide a helpful framework for us as we help others reflect on their life and practice of ministry. The ultimate goal of all spiritual direction or Christian coaching is to help others reflect on their practices so they can respond faithfully to God's call in every area of their life.

WHERE SPIRITUAL FORMATION HAPPENS

David Thornburg, who has been described as the "premier futurist in educational technology" identifies in his book *From the Campfire to the Holodeck: Creating Engaging and Powerful 21st Century Learning Environments*, three archetypal learning spaces: the campfire, the cave, and the watering hole. Each space has a distinct function in human learning that corresponds directly to being a disciple and a learner. We believe that these spaces offer us primal insight that will help us reclaim healthy rhythms of leadership in the ordinary spaces of life in today's world.

The cave is the private space where we as individuals can think, reflect, and transform learning from external knowledge into internal belief. This space reminds us that personal, spiritual, and emotional health comes from having a healthy balance of retreat and engagement (the ebb and flow we talked about in Part One). The cave, in other words, is where we create sacred space to be alone with God and develop the art of spiritual reflection.

The campfire is the space where people gather to learn from an expert. In the days of old, wise elders passed down insights through storytelling, and in so doing, replicated culture for the next generation. This space reminds us of the importance of being and having coaches and mentors in our lives. I (Winfield) often tell people that we all need a Gandalf, someone who can speak into our lives. This is where having a spiritual director or a coach is so important for leadership development.

Finally, *the watering hole* is the informal space where peers can share information and discoveries, acting as both learner and teacher simultaneously. This shared space can serve as an incubator for ideas and can promote a sense of shared culture. We believe that the waterhole is where creating a coaching culture becomes a reality.

Imagine if leaders everywhere, in churches, businesses, or organizations embodied the rhythms we have discussed throughout this book in their daily lives. Imagine a world in which leaders led out of a place of health and vitality instead of from burnout, fear, or scarcity. Imagine, if they took time to care for their own souls and to lead others in how to live healthy rhythms as well. Imagine if churches, non-profits, and businesses were places of spiritual health and healing, living not for their own interests but for the sake of the world. It has been said that if we want to see change in the world, it has to begin with us. It starts with us—including you!

CLOSING PRAYER

Dear Lord, who leads and guides us in the way of truth,
Teach me how to be a spiritual guide for others.
Speak to my hearts about how to prayerfully guide others in the
way of Jesus.
Let your will be done in our families, our churches, our cities, our
nation, and our world.
Lead us, and guide us as we seek to guide others. Amen.

ESSENTIAL THOUGHT

Being a spiritual guide for others in the Way involves four core competencies: praying, listening, asking questions, and reflecting.

Practice

Make notes of which of the four core competencies you need to practice. If truth be told, many of us need to develop the skill of active listening. Try actively listening to someone without feeling the need to respond. Intentionally spend time practicing these skills over a period of time until "listening deeply" becomes something you do automatically.

Chapter 7

STARTING SOUL CARE GROUPS

"If you want to go fast, go alone; but if you want to go far, go together."

– AFRICAN PROVERB

One of the dangers of reading a book like this on soul care is to that you may make the mistake of thinking that you can do it on your own. Nothing could be farther from the truth. The facts are out: leaders are lonely. As we have already seen, one of the biggest contributing factors for leadership burnout is loneliness. It was never intended to be this way; in fact, God has created us for fellowship, not to be alone. Fellowship is an intimate union in which Christians share. This is not just a friendship but also a deep bond that only Christians can know within the family of God. At the heart of the Greek word for fellowship (*koinonia*) is the idea of participation in life together. No single word in the English language captures the beautiful meaning of this word. When reading the book of Acts, we can see that the life of the early church revolved around this type of community and fellowship. Acts 2:42 says, "They devoted themselves to the

> Fellowship is an intimate union in which Christians share.

apostles' teaching and to fellowship, to the breaking of bread and to prayer."

There is a rich tradition in the church called the "cure of souls." The cure of souls (*cura animarum* in Latin), refers to the pastoral practice of caring for souls that was exercised by a priest. This included things such as preaching, confession, sacraments, spiritual direction, and visitation. However, while this term has historically referred to the work that is done primarily by a professional clergy person in pastoring their congregants, it can also be applied to the work that Christians can do for one another in Soul Care Groups. We believe that the work of soul care is best done in context of community. Simply put, we need the whole body of Christ to be made whole, not just a priest.

In this final chapter, we explore the importance of small group discipleship (what we're calling Soul Care Groups) and offer a framework that will help you develop an intentional and adaptable process for connecting people into these groups. Soul Care Groups are an important way to help people build authentic communities of faith that encourage spiritual formation and inner transformation.

SMALL DISCIPLESHIP

Small groups are nothing new. We can see dynamics of small group ministry in the life and ministry of Jesus Christ as he spent time teaching his twelve disciples. A closer look at the Gospels, however, reveals that Jesus spent additional time developing Peter, James, and John, who might as well be considered the inner circle of the original twelve disciples. Here we see small groups at work in Jesus' discipleship methodology.

We also see the importance of small groups through the book of Acts and in the rest of the New Testament. In fact, many of the letters were written to churches that met in ordinary peoples' homes. We see in the Bible how disciples are made through building a biblical, Christ-centered community. When reading the book of Acts, we can see that the life of the early church revolved around community that happened in small group gatherings in homes. Community is an intimate union in which Christians can share their life together in fellowship.

While there are many historic examples of small group discipleship, the first example is the Celtic Christians movement that began with Saint Patrick in Ireland. What made the Celt movement unique is that they did evangelism and discipleship as a team, instead of as individuals. This means they didn't go out and try to win the world by themselves; rather they went out as a team because they understood the power of numbers. Each member of the Celtic missionary team played an important role in the whole effort of reaching the community. Author John Finney observes that the Celts believed in "the importance of the team. A group of people can pray and think together. They inspire and encourage each other. The single entrepreneur is too easily prey to self-doubt and loss of vision."[67] The Celtic "team approach" to ministry and discipleship is an important alternative to the modern lone ranger mentality that is typical in many Western churches. We desperately need to recover the team approach.

The Celtic Christians entered into the community they were trying to reach with the gospel, where they lived, worked, and ate—where they spent time with the people they were trying to reach. This is contrary to the way most modern Christians try to reach people. Whereas they went to where the people were, we usually expect people to come to us. They knew that God created man to live in community with others. In the context of Christian community, spiritual seekers were able to explore the faith in real-life settings. They saw the gospel message lived out before them. In this sense, Christian community is a living sacrament that demonstrates the eternal truths of the Word of God.

The Celtic Christians developed a holistic approach to discipleship that prepared people to live out their faith with a sense of depth, compassion, and power in mission. The Celtic believers were immersed in a holistic spirituality that was characterized by depth and meaning, and enabled them to withstand difficulty and hardships in their everyday lives. In other words, their faith wasn't just theoretical but practical and relevant to everyday life.

One of the major problems in many discipleship approaches is that leaders' efforts are one-dimensional. Many Christians see themselves through only one lens (as either evangelical, sacramental, charismatic, etc.). However, like a diamond, the Christian faith offers multiple dimensions, and the Celtic Christians understood this complex nature of the faith. They sought to bring together a faith encounter that encouraged spiritual growth on many levels. George Hunter recounts how they had a four-fold structure of experiences that deepened their faith. Hunter says:

> 1. You experienced voluntary periods of solitary isolation in a remote natural setting (i.e., a grove of trees near a stream where you can be alone with God).

2. You spent time with your "soul friend," a peer with whom you were vulnerable and accountable, to whom you made confession, and from whom you received absolution and penance. You both supported and challenged you.

3. You spent time with a small group.

4. You participated in the common life, meals, work, learning, biblical recitation, prayers and worship with the whole Christian community.[68]

Through having a small group and living in community life believers observed and gained experience in ministry and witness to unchurched people.

Another one of our favorite historic examples, which we often point people to, is the discipleship structure of the Wesleyan revival of the 18th century. John Wesley organized the early Methodists into three types of discipleship groups: societies, class meetings, and band meetings.[69] While the societies used to gather people in larger numbers for teaching and edification and the class meetings of ten to twelve people provided space for more in depth discipleship, Wesley favored the band meeting because of its smaller size of three to five people. He believed the band provided the best potential for spiritual growth and development because of the intimate size of the group. While the band was smaller than the class, it carried with it more rigorous requirements, offered more intimate structure, and led to increased mutual encouragement.

The bands were divided by gender and marital status, and they were designed to provide a forum in which the members of the group could confess their sins, then encourage and pray for one another. For many contemporary Christians, the intimacy and accountability of the band meeting might seem a little intense, even intrusive. According to professors Kevin Watson and Scott T. Kisker, "The honesty and integrity of the bands is tremendously rare in our culture, even within the contemporary church. Through them God ministered sanctifying grace in intimate space."[70] The band meeting was a place where many of the Methodist leaders were formed.

The rules of the band were as follows:

The design of our meeting is to obey that command of God, "Confess your sins to each other and pray for each other so that you may be healed" (James 5:16). To this end, we intend:

- To meet once a week, at the least.
- To come punctually at the hour appointed, without some extraordinary reason.
- To begin (those who are present) exactly at the hour, with singing or prayer.
- To speak each of us in order, freely and plainly, the true state of our souls, with the faults we have committed in thought, word, or deed, and the temptations we have felt since our last meeting.
- To end every meeting with prayer suited to the state of each person present.
- To desire some person among us to speak his own state first, and then to ask the rest, in order, as many and as searching questions as may be, concerning their state, sins, and temptations.[71]

This short account gives us a glimpse into what it was like to participate in one of the meetings. Wesley wanted the members of a band to show constant progress in their walk with the Lord, and through the grace of God, these groups provided structure and relationships that fostered this progress.

In *The Band Meeting: Rediscovering Relational Discipleship in Transformational Community,* Kevin Watson opens up about his own personal experience being involved in a band:

> My first experience with a band meeting was the most profound experience of intimacy and vulnerability I had ever had up until that point. It was the first time I was invited that deeply into other men's lives. Being in that group helped me begin to tell the truth about my own life, especially the places where I was stuck in shame. It was not easy. But it was extremely powerful. That group exposed an unexamined lie I had believed: if anyone really knew me, they could never love me. In that band meeting, as we snuck off to an empty classroom to eat lunch together and confess sin, I began to risk letting people know me. By the grace of God, I discovered I was not alone. Someone else could know me as I was, and love me. And God's grace could bring lasting healing and transformation.[72]

After reading Kevin's account and hearing him share his story on stage at a recent conference, I (Winfield) felt a conviction that my own life lacked the depth of relationship Kevin was experiencing with others, so I made a decision to join a band myself. I began meeting with a group of men in my neighborhood. Each week we come together to ask hard questions of each other and pray for one another. I am thankful God has put these men in my life and that I have a place every week where I can answer the question, "How is it with your soul?"

We love this size group because anyone can do it. The band meeting format can be used and adapted to any context. It doesn't take money or elaborate training, just three to five people who are willing to meet each week and ask deep spiritual questions. When the pandemic began to spread in the spring of 2020, our band went straight to Zoom and we haven't missed a week yet!

WHAT ARE SOUL CARE GROUPS?

We want to share with you now how you can start a Soul Care Group, which is built around the band meeting model. A typical Soul Care Group is made up of three to five people who meet every week to share, pray, and support one another. Soul Care Groups provide a place for spiritual growth, intimacy, accountability, and protection. There can be a Soul Care Group for everyone regardless of members' age, gender, or ethnicity, and you can start them anywhere. Pastors can use them in their churches; business leaders can start them at work; and college students can start them in their dorm rooms. Groups can meet in homes, coffee houses, backyards, bars, gyms, or anywhere else you can think of.

One leader usually leads, but there can also be several people who help lead the group. Since it is not a Bible study, you don't have to train people to teach. The average meeting lasts an hour to an hour and a half and can happen either in person or on online. The people that we connect with in Soul Care Groups community groups become our spiritual family that

The people that we connect with in Soul Care Groups community groups become our spiritual family

supports and encourages us. Through the true fellowship that can happen in a Soul Care Group, we experience and share the love of God with our brothers and sisters in Christ. In Soul Care Groups, we also become a part of the spiritual formation journey of others through the blessing of fellowship.

WHY BE PART OF A SOUL CARE GROUPS?

We've found specific benefits for those in a Soul Care Group. First, anyone can be a part of them. Soul Care Groups don't require a Ph.D. for membership, only a willingness to go deep with one another. This is what we most love about these groups, and it makes them easy to create and reproduce. Simply use the spiritual practices that we have highlighted in the book as a framework for your group.

Second, Soul Care Groups, are a place for believers to live out their faith in community and to encourage one another in practicing the spiritual disciplines. The Christian faith is a social religion, not a solitary one. To many people feel isolated and desperate for community, and Soul Care Groups are an easy and effective way to connect people in community.

Third, Soul Care Groups are free and don't cost anything— and they don't even require curriculum. All you need is three to five people to make them happen. The key word here is *free*; they don't cost anything.

Fourth, Soul Care Groups are a place for believers to pray for one another. Prayer is one of God's greatest gifts that he has given the church, yet we seldom pray for one another. Soul Care Groups provide a place for leaders to allow people to show down and prayer for one another.

Finally, Soul Care Groups are a place of accountability to confess our sins and share our struggles with others. We call this the gift of confession. As we confess our sins and struggles to one another, we can experience God's forgiveness and healing that is so needed in today's world.

WHAT SOUL CARE GROUPS ARE NOT

Let's take a minute to talk about what Soul Care Groups are not. If you are like us, you have probably had a bad small group experience at least once in your life. You know, the kind where someone takes over the discussion or where the leader allows too much time of awkward silence. There is nothing worse for cultivating community than a bad small group experience. In fact, this is the reason why so many people are reluctant to be a part of a small group. As group leaders, our job is to protect our small groups and make them a safe place for people to share, grow, and learn together. We want to encourage you to watch out for the following five landmines, each of which can destroy a good small group dynamic.

1. A Gossip Group. Soul Care Groups are not a place to talk about others; rather they should be a safe place free from gossip and condemnation. People who attend a Soul Care Groups should feel free to come as they are and share openly and honestly. If we are not careful, Soul Care Groups can degenerate into a gossip group that tears down instead of builds up.

2. A One-person Show. The leader should not do all the talking. Encourage others to participate and share in group discussions. In the past, I (Winfield) have been to some small groups where only one person does all the talking. When this happens, no one wants to share, much less attend. An effective

Soul Care Groups leader encourages everyone to participate in the times of discussion.

3. A Place to Complain About the Church. Soul Care Groups must not become a sounding board for disgruntled people to complain about the church. This is not a place to complain about and slander the church. If people have a problem with the church, they need to share it with the church's leadership, which is the biblical model (see Matt. 18:15). Train your leaders to protect the unity of the church by not allowing upset people to use the Soul Care Groups as a place to complain about their problems with others.

4. A Place for People to Take Over. Small groups can attract people who will hijack the group if you let them. Do not allow people to get off the subject by chasing rabbit trails. Whenever people start getting off track in the discussions, bring them back quickly. This requires a lot of discernment and grace. A good leader can keep people on track and the discussion moving.

5. An End in Themselves. Small groups must not become a social club, which is an end in itself. Instead, Soul Care Groups can be missional and should be a place that encourages the group to reach out to the world in fresh mission. Encourage the people in your community group to reach out to others. Begin thinking of creative ways you can serve together as a Soul Care Groups and be a blessing to the community where you live.

THREE SIMPLE QUESTIONS

What we love about Soul Care Groups is how simple and easy they are. You can implement one in any context. We put together five simple questions we adapted from Wesley's original band meeting questions that address five key areas of concern.

These questions can be adapted to meet the needs of the people in a given group. For instance, you can focus on two or three of the questions, or use all five! Feel free to take them and use them in any way that works best for you and your group.

1. SOUL

How is it with your soul?

2. STRUGGLES

Are there any sins, omissions, or shortcomings you need to confess?

3. SPIRIT

What do you sense the Holy Spirit doing in your life?

It's that simple! Why not try it? All you need is three to five people to begin. Regardless of what you call your group, discipleship groups like the Soul Care Groups can be an effective and simple way for making disciples today. The Bible provides no evidence of a lone ranger in the body of Christ. Serious discipleship efforts that grow people into spiritual maturity necessarily involves the whole body of Christ. We need to recognize the importance of meeting together with other Christians to share our experiences, hold one another accountable, and pray for one another, not to mention encouraging one another as we individually practice the spiritual disciplines.

Spiritual formation is best done in community with other Christians.

The goal of the Soul Care Group is to help Christians grow together in the faith and knowledge of the Lord Jesus Christ. Growing in our relationship with the Lord Jesus requires the type of interdependence with fellow believers that these groups offer. Soul Care Groups remind us that the ongoing practice of spiritual formation is best done in community with other Christians. Discipleship doesn't just happen. We need one another. This means that the Christian faith is more than a theory that is taught in a classroom, but something that is practiced in community with others.

CLOSING PRAYER

Dear Lord, you have created us for fellowship and community.
We thank you for the gift of fellowship, and may we who gather
together in this small group gather with other Christians for
mutual prayer, support, and encouragement.
Unite us together in the bonds of fellowship and use our group as a
means of grace that we may draw closer to you. Amen.

ESSENTIAL THOUGHT

A Soul Care Group is made up of three to five people who meet every week to share, pray, and support one another.

Put It into Practice

Start a Soul Care group with three or five people you know. If you are already a part of a small group, think about how you can implement some of the practices mentioned in this chapter. If you are a leader, consider starting Soul Care Groups in your church, at work, or in your neighborhood.

THE JOURNEY CONTINUES

You can't go back and change the beginning, but you can start where you are and change the ending.

- C.S. LEWIS

(Mark) grew up in Northern Ireland during turbulent times called "The Troubles" which refers to sectarian strife that erupted nearly forty years ago between Catholic and Protestants. More than 3,500 people were killed and thousands more were injured, some maimed for life. An inspiration for me was a small group of ladies who walked to a small church in Belfast every week to have a Bible study and to pray for peace in Northern Ireland. Today, this story might not have much meaning, but in the 1980s, when I was growing up, the nightly news in Ireland was filled with messages about how hopeless life in our small country was.

Even though we were loved by the whole world, we seemed caught in an endless cycle of mindless violence and hopelessness. Every day there was bad news: a soldier lost their life, a police officer was blown to pieces, a terrorist ambushed, a worker shot on their way to work. Life was far from normal in those days, and the lack of hope in our beautiful, wee country was in short supply. Yet, I was fascinated with these women and why they walked to church every week to study Scripture and pray together.

On their walk to the church, they most likely saw buildings burning. They would have heard sirens screaming or watched another mother on the nightly news who lost her son or daughter to the violence crying. They were probably stopped at an army check post as a young soldier's eyes—filled with fear as he pointed a gun in their face—looked at them and ask them where they were going. While most of the people in Northern Ireland at the time could not easily imagine a peaceful future, these ladies knew peace would come, and their faith instructed them to put their hope in meeting and praying together. This faith was well placed, because in 1996, Northern Ireland's politicians signed a historic peace agreement that lasts until today. The hope of these ladies is the reason that I still believe that the church has a role to play in today's society.

Though these church ladies surely faced personal adversity during their life journey, they were able to inspire realistic hope in others from the conviction of their faith. Looking back, I now understand the personal stories of these dear women and of many others throughout my life, who have inspired me to reconcile what is—with what could be. This book reflects our belief that a hopeful future for the church and world is possible. We have a realistic hope.

Today, our hope is not in great institutions, but in people— ordinary, everyday people. More specifically our hope is in leaders: faithful women and men who are serving others on the front lines every day. Leaders like you. You are the reason we wrote this book. We believe in you. The world needs leaders who are leading

Our hope is not in great institutions, but in people— ordinary, everyday people

out of a place of emotional and spiritual health that comes from being rooted and grounded in healthy rhythms. We believe that the rhythms and practices that we have discussed in the book will help you and those you are called to serve. We sincerely hope and pray that the contents of this book will equip and empower you and those you serve to develop healthy rhythms in these uncertain times.

Throughout the book, we have introduced you to various spiritual rhythms that are designed to help you cultivate soul care in your own life, including spiritual breathing, an Ebb and Flow Rule of Life and practicing the art of spiritual reflection. We have also offered tools and practices for navigating chaotic times, including leadership essentials, Design Thinking, and guiding others. For leaders, we hope that this book has also given you an adaptable framework that you can tend to the inner life of your soul and will help you become a spiritual guide for others you lead.

As we end the book, we want to offer a few next steps. First, put what you have read into practice. This is not an academic or theoretical book, but a book that is designed to put into practice. Many of these rhythms and practices take time to become natural, so stay at them until they become that way. The practices and principles in this book are not meant to be a straightjacket but to provide a structure that can be adapted to your daily life. You can use these in your life, your home, your family, and among those with whom you work and serve. Don't let it collect dust on a shelf. Read it and pass it on to others.

As we close, Godspeed to you as you continue on the journey!

A BLESSING FOR LEADERS

From Mark Dunwoody

May you know that history is not just in the past,
it is also in the present, and that you
carry history within you.

May your heart be imbued with a longing for beauty,
meaning, order, creativity, kindness, and love.

May you find the precious treasures of
your soul in the challenges you face.
May you have a sense of adventure as you
bring something new to the world.

May the flow of spiritual creativity, imagination,
and innovation wash over the
intimacy of your soul this day.

May the parched deserts of your heart be refreshed
by the waters of your baptism in Christ.
May you find a new beach in your heart
after the storms in your life.

May your kindness cast a different light over
the darkness and confusion of life—an evening
light—with a depth of color and patience to
illuminate what is complex and rich in diversity.

MISSIONAL FORMATION RESOURCES

To help leaders thrive today, we have developed resources to promote spiritual and emotional health. Whether it is in the market place or the church, we hope to help encourage and equip you to fulfil God's mission through our unique training, coaching, and resources.

WHAT WE DO

Alongside our podcast, The Missional Formation Podcast, we offer unique coaching and training courses in the following areas:

Missional Formation (Promoting Healthy Rhythms).

Missional Formation Coaching (Coaching and training).

Missional Innovation (Design Thinking).

Learn more at
www.missionalformationcoaching.com

Appendix

TOOLS FOR JOURNEY

LIST OF VALUES

Take time to go through the list of values and identify your top two to three core values. These values will help you prioritize the rhythms that you chose to put into your life. Then, after identifying your top two to three core values, spend time prayerfully creating a Rule of Life.

Accountability	Cooperation	Friendship
Achievement	Courage	Fun
Adaptability	Creation	Generosity
Adventure	Creativity	Giving
Altruism	Curiosity	Goodness
Balance	Dedication	Grace
Beauty	Dependability	Gratitude
Boldness	Determination	Growth
Bravery	Development	Happiness
Calmness	Dignity	Hard work
Caring	Discipline	Harmony
Charity	Discovery	Honesty
Comfort	Empathy	Honor
Commitment	Empower	Hope
Community	Endurance	Humility
Compassion	Enthusiasm	Humor
Confidence	Equality	Imagination
Connection	Ethical	Independence
Consistency	Excellence	Innovation
Contentment	Family	Insightful
Contribution	Fearless	Inspiring
Conviction	Focus	Integrity

Intelligence
Intensity
Intuitive
Joy
Justice
Kindness
Knowledge
Leadership
Learning
Liberty
Love
Loyalty
Maturity
Meaning
Motivation
Openness
Optimism
Organization
Originality
Passion
Patience
Peace
Perseverance
Presence
Purpose
Quality
Realistic
Reason
Recognition
Recreation
Reflective

Respect
Responsibility
Restraint
Reverence
Rigor
Risk
Selfless
Serenity
Service
Silence
Simplicity
Sincerity
Skill
Solitude
Spirit
Spontaneous
Stability
Stewardship
Strength
Sustainability
Talent
Teamwork
Thankful
Thoughtful
Timeliness
Tradition
Transparency
Trust
Truth
Understanding
Unity

Victory
Vision
Wisdom
Wonder

EBB AND FLOW RULE OF LIFE WORKSHEET

We crafted a Rule of Life that is divided into three categories: personal rhythms, leadership rhythms, and corporate rhythms. Take some time now on your own to pray over your Rule of Life. Start with identifying your core values and then fill in the various disciplines in a manner that make the most sense for your lifestyle.

CORE VALUES

1. _____ 2. _____ 3. _____

RHYTHMS	PERSONAL RHYTHMS	LEADERSHIP RHYTHMS	CORPORATE RHYTHMS
Daily			
Weekly			
Monthly			
Annually			

SPIRITUAL DISCIPLINES THAT CORRESPOND TO OUR NEEDS

The following is from Ruth Haley Barton's book
Sacred Rhythms.[73]

One way to become more intentional about our spiritual
rhythms is to choose spiritual practices and relationships
appropriate to the particular sins and negative patterns that
God is helping us become aware of . . . . Our arrangement of
spiritual practices and relationships becomes more personal as
we choose disciplines that correspond to those areas where we
recognize our specific need for spiritual transformation. The
following list is not exhaustive but offers a few examples to help
you begin looking at the spiritual disciplines in this way.

NEGATIVE PATTERNS	A CORRESPONDING DISCIPLINE
Gossip/Sins of speech	Silence, self-examination
Anxiety and worry	Breath prayer, Scripture reflection
Envy and competitiveness	Solitude, self-examination
Discontent	Attending to desire
Self-reliance	Silence, prayer, community
Avoidance patterns	Community, spiritual friendship
Over-busyness	Solitude, discernment, Sabbath, rule of life
Anger and bitterness	Silence, self-examination, confession

Feelings of inadequacy	Examen, self-knowledge and Celebration
Guilt, shame	Solitude, confession, forgiveness
Lust	Attending to desire in God's presence
Restlessness and stress	Solitude, silence, breath prayer
Lethargy and/or laziness	Caring for the body, exercise
Lack of faith	Prayer, scripture
Feelings of isolation	Examen of consciousness, community
Selfishness and self-centeredness	Prayer and worship in community
Lack of direction	Discernment, listening to the body

NOTES

1. Andy Crouch, Kurt Keilhacker, and Dave Blanchard, "Leading Beyond the Blizzard: Why Every Organization Is Now a Startup," https://journal.praxislabs.org/leading-beyond-the-blizzard-why-every-organization-is-now-a-startup-b7f32fb278ff.

2. Dallas Willard, *The Great Omission: Reclaiming Jesus's Essential Teachings on Discipleship* (San Francisco: HarperCollins, 2014), 122.

3. Barbara L. Peacock, *Soul Care in African American Practice* (Downers Grove, IL: IVP, 2019), 6.

4. Henri Nouwen, *In the Name of Jesus: Reflections on Christian Leadership* (New York: Crossroad Publishing Company, 1989), 20.

5. Alan and Eleanor Kreider, *Worship and Mission After Christendom* (Scottsdale, PA: Herald Press, 2011).

6. Henri Nouwen, *Out of Solitude: Three Meditations on the Christian Life* (Notre Dame, IN: Ave Maria Press, 2004), 17.

7. John Ronald Reuel Tolkien, *The Lord of the Rings* (United States: Houghton Mifflin, 2002), 32.

8. The earliest and most accurate account of the life and ministry of St. Aidan comes from the British historian Bede (672–735 A.D.) who lived shortly after Aidan's time. Bede, *A History of the English Church and People* (London: Penguin Classics, 1968), 149.

9. Ibid.

10. Ray Simpson and Brent Lyons-Lee, *St. Aidan Way of Mission: Celtic Insights for a Post-Christian World* (Oxford: The Bible Reading Fellowship, 2016) and Edward L. Smither, *Missionary Monks: An Introduction to the History and Theology of Missionary Monasticism* (Eugene, OR: Cascade Books, 2016), 64–81.

11. Ibid, 144 and 149.

12. Ibid, 148.

13. Ibid, 169.

14. Ibid, 98.

15. M. Robert Mulholland, *Invitation to a Journey: A Road Map for Spiritual Formation* (Downers Grove, IL: Intervarsity Press, 1993), 12.

16. "Marks of Mission," Anglican Communion, accessed February 25, 2021, http://www.anglicancommunion.org/mission/marks-of-mission.aspx.

17. Marcus Borg and N. T. Wright, *The Meaning of Jesus: Two Visions* (San Francisco: Harper Collins, 1999), 207.

18. Martin Luther King Jr., *Why We Can't Wait* (New York: Signet Books, 1964), 61.

19. Desmond Tutu, *God Has a Dream: A Vision of Hope for Our Time* (New York: Double Day, 2004), 101.

20. David Cole, *The Mystic Path of Meditation: Beginning as Christ-centered Journey* (UK: Harding House, 2013).

21. Steve Harper, *A Pocket Guide to Prayer* (Nashville: Upper Room, 2010), 7.

22. Richard Foster, *Celebration of Discipline: The Path to Spiritual Growth*, anniversary special edition (New York: HarperOne, 2018).

23. Peter Scazzero, *Emotionally Healthy Spirituality* (Grand Rapids, MI: Zondervan, 2006), 198–210.

24. Brené Brown, *Dare to Lead: Brave Work, Tough Conversations, Whole Hearts* (New York: Random House, 2018), 187.

25. Ibid. 187.

26. Ibid, 189.

27. Stephen A. Macchia, *Crafting a Rule of Life: An Invitation into the Well-Ordered Way* (Downers Grove, IL: InterVarsity Press, 2012), 17.

28. Howard Thurman, *Meditations of the Heart* (Richmond, Indiana: Beacon Press, 1999), 28.

29. Angela Wilkinson and Betty Sue Flowers, *Realistic Hope: Facing Global Challenges* (Amsterdam University Press, 2018).

30. Megan Hyatt Miller, "Why Hopeful Realism Beats Mandatory Optimism," https://michaelhyatt.com/hopeful-realism/.

31. Prior to the COVID-19 pandemic, Lifeway Research revealed that 23 percent of pastors acknowledge they have personally struggled with a mental illness and 49 percent say they rarely or never speak to their congregation about mental illness. Another Lifeway Research study of pastors concluded that 84 percent say they are on-call 24 hours a day and 54 percent find the role of pastor frequently overwhelming. Combined with the COVID-19 pandemic and the massive logistical, relational, and financial pressures churches now face, leaders are experiencing significant challenges. For more information, visit the newly-formed Resilient Church Leadership Initiative at https://resilientchurchleadership.com/. We also recommend Jimmy Dodd with PastorServe, who has written several helpful books for pastors including, *Survive or Thrive: 6 Relationships Every Pastor Needs* (2015)

and *Pastors Are People Too: What They Won't Tell You but You Need to Know* (2016). See also, Scott Sauls, *From Weakness to Strength: 8 Vulnerabilities That Can Bring Out the Best in Your Leadership* (2017).

32. Peter Scazzero, *The Emotionally Healthy Leader: How Transforming Your Inner Life Will Deeply Transform Your Church, Team, and the World* (Grand Rapids, MI: Zondervan, 2015), 33.

33. Ibid.

34. Peter Scazzero, *Emotionally Healthy Spirituality: Unleash a Revolution in Your Life in Christ* (Nashville: Thomas Nelson, 2014), 45.

35. John Calvin, *Institutes of the Christian Religion*, vol. 1 (Grand Rapids, MI: Eerdmans Publishing Company, 1957), 37. See also David G. Benner, *The Gift of Being Yourself: The Sacred Call to Self-Discovery* (Downers Grove, IL: IVP Books, 2015).

36. Travis Bradberry and Jean Greaves, *Emotional Intelligence 2.0* (San Diego: Talent Smart, 2009), 17.

37. Edwin Friedman, *A Failure of Nerve: Leadership in an Age of the Quick Fix* (New York: Church Publishing, 2007), 15.

38. Martin Luther King Jr., *Strength to Love* (Philadelphia: Fortress Press, 1963), 114.

39. Matt Gavin, "5 Characteristics of a Courageous Leader," Harvard Business School Online, March 3, 2020, https://online.hbs.edu/blog/post/courageous-leadership. See also Nancy Koehn, *Forged in Crisis: The Making of Five Courageous Leaders* (New York: Scribner, 2018).

40. Brené Brown, *Dare to Lead: Brave Work, Tough Conversations, Whole Hearts* (New York: Random House, 2018), 20.

41. Cambridge Leadership Associates, https://cambridge-leadership.com/adaptive-leadership/.

There are a number of relevant resources that we would recommend for leaders on adaptive leadership. I (Winfield) have been blessed by being coached by J. R. Briggs, who coaches and helps leaders at https://www.kairospartnerships.org and recently wrote *The Sacred Overlap: Learning to Live Faithfully in the Space Between* (2020). See also Tod Bolsinger has two significant books on adaptive leadership including *Canoeing the Mountains: Christian Leadership in Uncharted Territory* (2018) and *Tempered Resilience: How Leaders Are Formed in the Crucible of Change* (2020).

See also Martin Linsky and Ron A. Heifetz, *Leadership on the Line: Staying Alive through the Dangers of Leading* (2002), and Martin Linsky, Ron A. Heifetz and Alexander Grashow, *The Practice of Adaptive Leadership* (2009).

42. Leonard Sweet, *AquaChurch* (Loveland, CO: Group, 1999), 8.

43. George G. Hunter III, *The Recovery of a Contagious Methodist Movement* (Nashville: Abingdon Press, 2011), 28.

44. Gary Collins, *Christian Coaching* (Colorado Springs, CO: NavPress, 2002), 316.

45. David Littlemore, *Cultural Intelligence: Youth, Family, and Culture* (Grand Rapids, MI: Baker Academic, 2009).

46. A number of secular leadership thinkers have recognized the importance of servant leadership. See Simon Sinek, *Leaders Eat Last: Why Some Teams Pull Together and Others Don't* (2017); Ken Blanchard and Renee Broadwell, *Servant Leadership in Action: How You Can Achieve Great Relationships and Results* (2018); and Robert K. Greenleaf, *Servant Leadership: A*

Journey into the Nature of Legitimate Power and Greatness, 25th anniversary ed. (2002).

47. Henri Nouwen, *In the Name of Jesus* (New York: Crossroad Publishing Company, 1989), 63.

48. Richard Buchanan, "Wicked Problems in Design Thinking," *Design Issues* 8, no. 2 (Spring 1992): 5–21.

49. Ibid.

50. Peter Ball introduces readers to spiritual direction in the Anglican tradition and looks at some of the leading figures from the past to illustrate the roots and development of Anglican spiritual direction, including George Herbert, Lancelot Andrewes, John Wesley, Somerset Ward, and Evelyn Underhill. Plus, Ball mentions more recent influences in the revival of interest in the subject, like Kenneth Leech, Alan Jones, Gordon Jeff, and Margaret Guenther. See Peter Ball, *Anglican Spiritual Direction* (Harrisburg: Morehouse Pub., 2007).

51. Margaret Guenther, *Holy Listening: The Art of Spiritual Direction* (New York: Cowley Publications, 1992), xiii.

52. Ibid.

53. For a helpful article on how spiritual direction is being conducted in an African context, see Neal Siler, "The Efficacy of Spiritual Direction in the African American Christian Community," *Journal of Spiritual Formation & Soul Care* 10, no. 2 (2017): 304–312 and Puleng Matsaneng, "Spiritual Direction in Africa: A Need for a Different Approach?" *The Way* 49, no. 3 (July 2010): 53–64.

54. Henri Nouwen, *In the Name of Jesus* (New York: Crossroad Publishing Company, 1989), 42.

55. Thomas Merton, *Spiritual Direction and Meditation* (Collegeville, MN: The Liturgical Press, 1959), 28.

56. John Stott, *The Contemporary Christian: An Urgent Plea for Double Listening* (Leicester: InterVarsity Press, 1992), 29.

57. Margaret Guenther, *Holy Listening: The Art of Spiritual Direction* (London: Darton, Longman & Todd, 1993), 24.

58. John Swinton and Harriet Mowat, *Practical Theology*, second ed. (London: SCM Press, 2016), 6.

59. Richard R. Osmer, *Practical Theology: An Introduction* (Grand Rapids, MI: Wm. B. Eerdmans Publishing Co., 2008), 5.

60. Craig Dykstra and Dorothy C. Bass, "A Theological Understanding of Christian Practices," *Practicing Theology: Beliefs and Practices in Christian Life*, eds. Miroslav Volf and Dorothy C. Bass (Grand Rapids, MI: Wm. Eerdmans Publishing, 2002), 18.

61. Pete Ward, *Introducing Practical Theology: Mission, Ministry, and the Life of the Church* (Grand Rapids, MI: Baker Academic, 2017), 2–3.

62. Ibid, 5–6.

63. Ibid, 10.

64. Ibid, 24.

65. Ibid, 167–173.

66. Richard Osmer, *Practical Theology: An Introduction*, second ed. (London: SCM Press, 2016), 4.

67. John Finney, *Rediscovering the Past: Celtic and Roman Mission* (London: Darton, Longman, and Todd, 1996), 53.

68. George G. Hunter, *The Celtic Way of Evangelism: How Christianity Can Reach the West Again* (Nashville: Abingdon Press, 2010), 48.

69. For more on the Wesleyan discipleship structure, see Winfield Bevins, *Marks of a Movement: What the Church Today*

Can Learn from the Wesleyan Revival (Grand Rapids, MI: Zondervan, 2019).

70. Kevin Watson and Scott T. Kisker, *The Band Meeting: Rediscovering Relational Discipleship in Transformational Community* (Franklin, TN: Seedbed Publishing, 2017), 77.

71. John Wesley, Albert C. Outler, Frank Baker, and Henry D. Rack, *The Works of John Wesley* (Oxford: Clarendon Press, 1975), 181.

72. Kevin M. Watson and Scott Thomas Kisker, *The Band Meeting: Rediscovering Relational Discipleship in Transformational Community* (Franklin, TN: Seedbed Publishing, 2017), 15.

73. Ruth Haley Barton, *Sacred Rhythms* (Downers Grove, IL: InterVaristy Press, 2006), 186–187.

ABOUT THE AUTHORS

Winfield Bevins is an author and teacher whose passion is to help others connect to the roots of the Christian faith for spiritual formation and mission. He is the Director of Church Planting at Asbury Theological Seminary and co-founder of Missional Formation Coaching. As a seasoned practitioner he has helped start several churches and non-profit organizations. He frequently speaks at conferences on a variety of topics and is a guest lecturer at various seminaries and universities. He is a sought-after missional coach and consultant for churches, denominations, and networks in various global contexts. In addition to his work as a teacher and a coach, he is the author of numerous books including Ever Ancient Ever New and Marks of a Movement. You can connect with him at winfieldbevins. com and on twitter @winfieldbevins.

Mark Dunwoody has more than three decades of international experience as an entrepreneur and consultant to non-profits and faith communities. Originally from Belfast, Ireland, Mark has lived in five countries and is well known, internationally, in the missional conversation as a writer, trainer, speaker, strategist, and coach. While living in Canada, he was the leader of the Fresh Expressions Canada Church Planting movement. Mark also has led an NGO that has provided sustainable water, medical, and education solutions for rural communities since 2006 in Uganda, Africa. Mark is the co-founder of Missional Formation Coaching.